The Coach's Coach

The Coach's Coach
Lewis Joseph D'Antoni

ISBN: 978-0-557-53050-2

Written for Andrea's Great Grandchildren and my Grandchildren – Andrew, Bailey, Kennedy, Matthew, Michael, Morgan, Nicholas, and Parker and the future D'Antoni generation

A Special Thank You to Jeanie Houck Edwards, Sally Finchum and Stephanie Lilly

Contents

Foreword

My daughter, Kathy, convinced me to write my autobiography. She assured me that my great-grandchildren, grandchildren, and, yes, even my children would cherish these recollections, and that there may even be others who would be interested in reading my story. So, with little talent and some skepticism, I agreed.

I am a first-generation American, born to Italian immigrants. My parents were extremely poor and—like many immigrants—they came to America because they had dreams for themselves and their children. They were born in the town of Campi, in the province of Norcia and the region of Umbria, Italy. Andrea, my dad, was born December 26, 1888, to Adamo and Barbara Vancelli D'Antoni. Fiordoliva, my mother, was born October 17, 1893, to Luigi and Speranza Cameresi.

My story spans more than a century and is written for my family, their families, my eight grandchildren, and anyone else with an interest in my thoughts and opinions on life and sports in the twentieth century.

Chapter One:

Background

Sitting with my family in a quaint restaurant in Rye, New York, on December 31, 2008, I smiled when Morgan, my granddaughter, remarked, "Wow, Paw Paw, that's a lot of candles!" Morgan was surveying the ninety-five candles proudly stacked atop my birthday cake. *Wow is right*, I thought; *time isn't just marching on— it's in a full-court sprint.*

Being ninety-five, living alone in my brick house on Moran Avenue in Mullens, West Virginia, and occasionally playing a round of golf is somewhat of an oddity. Most folks who know my age usually start a conversation with the question, "How are you feeling?" or "How are you doing?"

My quick response is, "If you can tell me how a ninety-five-year-old should feel or be doing, then I will be happy to answer your question." Although my age is a dominant part of most conversations, wondering how long I will live or when I will die doesn't occupy my thoughts. Over the years, I have learned not to worry about what I can't control; I don't need to give it my precious time or thoughts. So, here I am, ninety-five years of age, and other than some minor physical irritations, my health is good. I am very fortunate to be blessed beyond my worth.

Writing this book forces me to reflect on my ninety-five years—almost a century—of life. Using the word "force" may seem odd, but I think there is a misconception about older folks sitting around reliving their lives and past experiences in today's society. I cannot speak for all seniors, but I make it a point not to think about yesterday or tomorrow; I concentrate on enjoying today. It works beautifully. Nevertheless, for this project, sharing my thoughts and memories required me to embark on honest reflection.

Everyone experiences life-changing events that guide the way they live. Sifting through old memories and tracing the pattern of my life, I can identify two prominent events that defined my storybook life. One is the day I asked Betty Jo Bailey to marry me, and the second is the moment I decided to become a basketball coach.

Comparing a person to an event may not be equal pairing, but these two passionate forces constantly intertwined throughout my life and gave me a great ride. Although Betty Jo is no longer with me and I am not presently able to physically participate in organized basketball events, both still permeate throughout my being and continue to be the pivotal forces in my life.

I had the pleasure of being Betty Jo's life escort for fifty-seven years. What a lady! She was beautiful, a first-class athlete, very competitive, self-assured, and daring. I was a somewhat shy Italian kid who lacked self-confidence; she was an extraverted, poised lady—my opposite personality type and exactly what I needed. Betty Jo, who was not afraid of the devil, was an independent woman, born years ahead of her time, and she continually supported my efforts, albeit in her own unique way.

One night when we were newlyweds, she woke me out of a deep sleep. "Lewis, Lewis, wake up! Someone's on the front porch and trying to break into the house."

I listened for a minute. "There's no one there," I said sleepily.

"Oh, yes, there is. I heard them. Come on, Lewis, get up and go see who's trying to break in."

Reluctantly, I climbed out of bed and started down the stairs. Betty Jo kept her target pistol in the drawer of the nightstand, so she grabbed the gun and followed close behind me. Now, let me state that I always thought the movie industry made a mistake when they did not cast a part for her in the movie, *Walking Tall*. She was never afraid to take justice into her own hands.

Halfway down the stairs, I turned around and headed back up. "Lewis," Betty Jo hissed, "where are you going?"

Unabashed, I replied, "Hell, Jo, with them in front of me and you behind me, I don't stand a chance. I'm going back to bed." I may have lacked self-confidence, but my common sense was definitely intact.

During the first years of our marriage, I coached three sports. There were numerous meetings to attend, and unfortunately, it meant arriving home late on many nights. Although Betty Jo did not complain, it bothered me when I had meetings three nights out of a week.

One night, Betty Jo was waiting for me to arrive home from a regional coaches meeting. To occupy her time while waiting, she decided to clean her target pistol, the one she kept in the nightstand drawer. She had just finished cleaning the gun when I drove into the driveway. Hearing my car, Betty Jo had a mischievous thought and decided to play a joke on me. Jumping up from the couch, gun in hand, she quickly turned off the lights and quietly waited for me in the dark. Entering through the side door, I carefully felt my way to the lamp sitting on the piano. As my hand reached for the light, Betty Jo jabbed the gun in my ribs and whispered, "I always wanted to kill you, you son of a bitch!" In a defensive reflex motion, I whirled around quickly while raising my arm and knocked her across the room. Peals of laughter filled the darkened room as Betty Jo fell backward onto the floor. Quickly turning on the light, with my knees shaking and insides churning, I saw Betty

Jo doubled over in laughter. She was holding the empty gun with its bullet chamber hanging open. Looking up at me, she laughingly said, "Glad you're home safe and sound, honey."

As these incidents attest, from the time we recited our marriage vows until the day I knelt beside her and promised to reunite in heaven, there was never a dull moment. Her large family—two brothers, six sisters, and a number of nieces and nephews—lived within ten miles of us. Add to that group our four children, and I assure you there was an on-going Grand Central Station-atmosphere at our house.

Our home in Mullens, a modest two-story brick, was built by my father in the early 1900s, and he gave it to us as a gift. When our children were young, the house was the site of constant activity, with Betty Jo in charge. She was a natural born politician, who made certain everyone entering our home knew they were a welcomed guest. Everyone congregated in the kitchen, the hub of all the comings and goings. No matter where you were stepping on the walk of life, in Betty Jo's kitchen, you were treated like royalty. Daily conversations between visitors, friends, and family members took place at the large, round oak table, while delicious Southern cooking and unending cups of coffee were served. If the kitchen walls could talk, scholars could research American history there. Discussions ran the gambit of major life-changing problems, to solving the United State's major economic problems, to politics, to reworking the educational system, to developing winning strategies for ball games, to the correct coaching strategies, to the proper way to raise children, and, most importantly, to what to prepare for dinner that night. Every conversation was as engaging and enlightening as the next one, and boring chitchat was nonexistent.

The kitchen was magical, filled with wonderful smells escaping from the simmering pots on the stove where lingering conversations permeated the air. Frequent visitors discovered it was a place where Santa Claus still chuckled, family get-togethers were exciting, and people genuinely cared about each other's happiness. I will be forever grateful to Betty Jo for giving me this type of foundation for building our strong family unit, a team that loved and worked together. This type of family just doesn't happen; it is very carefully cultivated and takes countless hours of devoted time. Ours happened because of Betty Jo.

The amazing thing about Betty Jo is that she gave me the gift of family even though I had, and still have, a lifelong mistress. My mistress's name is basketball. At times, my passion, my thoughts, and even my heart belonged to her. How and why my wife stayed with me when basketball continually consumed my time and attention remains a mystery. Surprisingly, Betty Jo not only stayed with me in light of my illicit indiscretions, but she wasn't even jealous (well, maybe a little perturbed at times). More than once she remarked that if she heard a ball bounce one more time, she would scream.

Throughout the years, Betty Jo was my mainstay and the primary reason for my successes. She was my love, and basketball was my lover. However, we did manage to have four wonderful children during timeouts.

These timeouts were also filled with family activities, worldly events, and discussions around the kitchen table, and coaching basketball was the main event. As I said, basketball was my passion. Over fifty-two years of coaching and playing and an additional thirty years of watching basketball games at all levels, coupled with living for ninety-five years, have given me adequate stories and an array of opinions to share. Everything in this book is written through my lens as a husband, father, and an experienced coach, especially everything about my life and about the greatest game of sports ever played: basketball.

Chapter Two:

Philosophical Thoughts

As people age, certain judgments come to light about the world they have experienced. I am no different. My opinions in this book range from my overall view on life to more specific subjects, and the one that interests me the most is basketball. To some, life and basketball may seem to be different philosophical venues, but in my mind, they are closely related, both by philosophy and by how they should be approached.

Philosophically, life and basketball are perpetual games with designated starting times and ending times. Each has specific rules, plays, coaches, teammates, referees, spectators, and sponsors. To be successful, one must utilize thoughtful preparation and give his or her best effort to avoid negative outcomes. There are strategically crafted wins, and there are other wins that are just lucky. Both basketball and life, at times, are not fair, but those who choose to continue to strive will ultimately succeed. Bottom line: the game of basketball is a microcosm of life, with valuable life lessons available for all students of the game.

Similarities between life and basketball not only exist philosophically, but also in their respective quests. As human beings, I would venture to say that most of us try to grab the proverbial brass ring, to work to reach our goals, to find our niche, and to strive to live the life that we think will bring us happiness. We look for answers that will help us achieve our dream, and each of us searches for an answer to our individual quest. I have a kinship with Billy Crystal when he was looking for life answers in the movie *City Slickers*. He asked Jack Palance, who was portraying a self-confident, hardened cowboy, "What is the secret to a happy life?" Most folks ask the same question that Crystal did and look for the answer that will provide them happiness.

Whether or not it's my gray hair or my aging spirit, similar questions are often asked of this experienced cowboy. People sometimes ask, "What is the secret to a successful life?" or, more specifically, "What is the secret to a successful basketball team?" Without hesitation, I confidently give the same answer: winning!

Before you get upset about my statement, let me explain the answer. Winning is set in different backdrops. One type of winning is defined in a public venue, such as having a winning sport season, earning winning records, being elected to public office, or setting a new record for company sales. To be successful in the public venue, a person must win. Not many bonuses are given to people for showing up and trying hard or given to coaches who produce mediocre seasons.

Then there's winning as defined in a personal venue, such as achieving one's goals, overcoming a bad trait or habit, or most importantly, enjoying the journey life offers you. Whatever the setting is public or personal, success ultimately is determined by the ability to win.

To me, the more important question is *how* to achieve a winning life or a winning basketball team. Numerous books have been written about the subjects but there have been no simple answers. Achieving success is complex; it involves a number of variables and a bit of luck. I do not profess to have the absolute answer to this question, but through my experiences and observations, it is evident that a winning life or a winning basketball team are both rooted in having a strong family unit. This unit, when properly developed, ultimately acts as a launching pad for success. To create one requires diligent work. Quite a bit of time must be spent on developing the positive relationships that develop deep personal ties, whether it is with kin (which includes, as Betty Jo would say, in-laws or outlaws), personal friends, or teammates. Moreover, the family members need to be united but not single-minded, to care deeply for each other but not blind to imperfections, to be supportive but not indulgent, to be close-knit but open to others, and, most importantly, to always be attuned to the whole. Families, lives, and teams that attain this level of unity produce winners, and, in later years, the family becomes a personal oasis for its members. For me, time has proven these principles to be true, and I am fortunate that as a coach and husband I have been the head of such families.

Chapter Three:

Andrea D'Antoni

It's early morning, 1978, and the sun, announcing the beginning of a new day, protrudes through the tailored curtains of my dad's darkened bedroom as Betty Jo enters carrying the morning newspaper. My father, diagnosed with bone cancer, is living with us. The cancer has progressed to its final stages, leaving him very weak and unable to leave the bed. His teary eyes slowly open as Betty Jo speaks. "Your name made the papers again, Mr. Dan." Lying in the bed, Dad reaches for the newspaper and takes it from her. His thin hands pull the front page close to his face, and he reads silently: D'ANTONI SHOOTS DOWN THE RUSSIANS. The Huntington newspaper had reported a story about an international basketball game that involved his grandson Mike and his Italian team. It reported that Mike scored a three-point basket at the buzzer to defeat the Russians. Slowly, Dad's arms lower, as they are too weak to hold the newspaper, and it slides to the floor. Betty Jo retrieves the paper, and while she quietly leaves the room, she notices a small, weak smile slowly spreading across Dad's tired face. Three days later, Andrea D'Antoni dies. He was eighty-nine.

Andrea's family, sitting quietly in the front of the small Catholic church where a flag-draped coffin graces the altar, listens as the priest praises Andrea D'Antoni, a father and grandfather. In the eulogy, the priest portrays him as an Italian immigrant. As I listen, a silent, burning question for the well-intended priest forms in my mind. Did you really know the man who died? I still remember that day in February 1978 and cannot reconcile the words of the priest with the deeds of my father. He did not think of himself as an immigrant. He was an American.

In my lifetime, I have not met anyone whose pride of being American equaled my father's. Every March 15, the day income taxes were due, Dad would celebrate the moment and, with great pride, write his income tax check to the United States government. It was his way of saying thank you for everything America had given him. Until the day he died, the ritual never changed. Dad never understood why people complained about paying taxes. He considered it a great privilege.

When my youngest son, Mark, was six years old, he witnessed Dad's ritual. It was April 15, 1970, and Andrea was sitting at the kitchen table with Mark nearby. As Dad finished signing his name to the bottom of the check, Andrea proudly opened a bottle of wine, lit a big cigar, and clapped his hands in celebration. He had performed this ritual for sixty-nine straight years, but this time it was in full view of his curious young grandson.

"Why are you so happy, Paw Paw?" Mark asked, watching his grandfather closely.

"It make me proud," Andrea boasted, "to pay back to my country for givin' me sucha good life. I make money; I raise four children; I have wonderful grandchildren." Andrea winked at his grandson. "I'ma happy and a proud man, and it's all because of my country, America."

"I'm an American, too. Aren't I, Paw Paw?" Mark remarked, anxious to be included in the happy moment.

"Yes, you are American." Andrea smiled. "But you musta never forget, you are also a D'Antoni. You must always be a good boy and make me proud, like your brothers, Danny and Mike."

Mark quickly responded, "I will Paw Paw, you'll see. I'll be good just like them."

Andrea beamed as he looked at his beautiful grandson. He was so proud of his family. All his children had been successful, and now his grandchildren promised to fulfill the vow he made the day he arrived in America.

It is rare for me to have a day pass without thinking about my father and mother, their journey, their accomplishments, and their hardships. My mind floods with childhood memories and family accounts and my father's prophecy for his family to become successful American citizens.

Andrea was the first member of his immediate family to emigrate to the United States. Campi, the small town in Italy where Andrea had lived, afforded little opportunity for its townspeople to earn a daily living, especially for a twenty-year-old. Andrea's life was difficult. His father was abusive, and as Andrea grew to manhood, the fights escalated. Madalena, Andrea's aunt, realized his future held little promise. The continuous fighting with his father and Andrea's inability to find work convinced Madalena that she had to find a way to get him out, to find him a place to live where he had a chance.

The Cameresis, former neighbors of Andrea's family, had immigrated to America two years earlier. Luigi Cameresi had brought his wife, mother, father, and his four children to America, where they settled in McComas, a small coal mining town in West Virginia. When they arrived at the coal camp, everyone in the family had to work. The Cameresis' home became a boarding house managed by Luigi's wife and their two daughters. Luigi and his sons worked in the coal mines. By working hard, each one contributed to the household earnings, and they did quite well financially. The news of their success in the new country traveled back to Campi.

Madalena wrote to them about Andrea and asked Luigi if he would agree to sponsor his visit to America. Understanding the young man's plight, Luigi agreed to be Andrea's sponsor. He invited him to stay at their boarding house until he had earned enough money to be on his own. Excited about the possibility, Madalena and Andrea began doing odd jobs—taking in laundry, cleaning homes, and any other job they could find—in order to get enough money to buy Andrea's passage to America.

In 1910, Andrea had the money for his passage and, like thousands of other western Europeans, he set sail for America. He boarded the ship *Germania* in Naples, Italy, bound for America. It was not unusual to have over six hundred immigrants crowded on board for the long trip from Italy to America. Andrea D'Antoni, a strapping and handsome young man of twenty-two, sailed in such conditions as he left home seeking a new life.

After spending several uncomfortable weeks at sea, he stepped off the crowded boat and stretched his legs, tying to adjust to walking on land. Unable to speak, read, or understand English, he anxiously awaited some sign as to where to go or what to do from the uniformed men who seemed to be the *funzionairi (bureaucratic official)*.

Other immigrants came off of the boat, and a large group of people started to assemble. "Form a line on the right," commanded a loud, sharp voice, breaking through the lively conversations. Andrea observed everyone moving to his right. He did not understand what the man had said, but the tone was unmistakably a command. Following an elderly man beside him, Andrea found his way into the line. Anxious, but youthfully unafraid, Andrea waited his turn to be admitted into the United States of America. Nothing, not the long trip, his inability to speak English, or even the uncertainty of being totally alone, could dampen his excitement and joy of being in the new country. Even at his young age, Andrea knew he was very lucky; he had a chance, a chance to live a good life.

Now he was actually on American soil, standing in line, trying to understand the loud commands from the official in front of him. "State your name and your purpose for being here!" barked the uniformed *funzionari,* who was sitting at a large table staring up at Andrea. "What's your name and why are you here?" he repeated.

Andrea stared at the man, trying to figure out what he was saying; finally, he shrugged his shoulders and shook his head in confusion. The *funzionari,* eventually understanding Andrea's problem, repeated the question in Italian. Eyes sparkling with excitement and comprehension, Andrea stated firmly in a proud voice, *"Il mio nome Andrea D'Antoni io voglio diventare un Americano!"* (My name is Andrea D'Antoni, and I want to be an American.)

No words have ever been truer than those spoken by my father that day. This was his new home, his new country, his new life. But suddenly, Dad felt ashamed. America was giving him everything, and he had nothing to give in return. All he had to offer the new country was himself. After a few minutes of serious deliberation, his spirits recovered. He thought of a gift worthy enough to give his country. On July 4, 1909, Andrea D'Antoni made a solemn vow that would be passed from D'Antoni generation to generation: his family name, D'Antoni, would always carry honor in America.

He was quickly processed by the immigration officials, who placed a large piece of white paper on the lapel of his coat. It had his destination, McComas, West Virginia, boldly printed in large letters. His new adventure in America had begun. Although he spoke no English, Andrea was filled with hope and pride as he left New York for West Virginia. He was reunited with Luigi Cameresi and his family in McComas, where he started work for the American Coal Company. He rented a room at the Cameresi's boarding house and was quite enamored with Luigi's youngest daughter, Fiordoliva, or Flora as she was known. It wasn't too long after Andrea's arrival that he and Flora Cameresi fell in love, and after a two-year courtship, the two were married on October 12, 1912. The newlyweds continued to live at the Cameresi's boarding house, as both families felt it would be financially prudent.

Anxious to start a family, Andrea dreamed of a son, a first-born son to carry the family name, the name that Andrea vowed would carry honor in America. The firstborn in Italian families holds elite ranking in the family unit, and the distinction is further enhanced if the firstborn is a son. To Andrea and Flora's delight, fourteen months later, on New Year's Eve, their first child arrived. They named him Luigi Giuseppe D'Antoni; I was their firstborn son.

Our small family continued to live at the boarding house for a couple of years until we moved into our own home, where we lived until I was six years old. My recollection of the McComas coal camp is very sketchy. The camp consisted of rows of small-framed houses that were owned by the coal company. The homes were occupied by families who had emigrated from Western Europe: Italians, Hungarians, Irish, all eagerly starting new lives in America. Our house was sparsely furnished, with just the necessities, and no indoor plumbing. Families shared outhouses that were built over nearby creeks. The roads were unpaved, no sidewalks existed, and a large coke oven stood at the end of every row of houses. Coke, not the fizzy drink, is a smokeless fuel made from bituminous coal and is perfect for use in heating stoves or furnaces. All the families living in that row shared the coke oven. The ovens were the perfect gathering place for mothers who met while baking bread, and they shared their families' stories and discussed daily events.

Another communal event that encouraged camp unity was the annual hog killing, which was held every fall. Folks would clean the hog and package all its parts, with each family sharing the meat. The hog was picked clean, and everything was used—that is, everything except the squeal.

My parents dreamed of the future. They worked hard so they could open their own business and raise a large family. Dad's first job at American Coal was the arduous job of picking bone from coal cars. Bone, an inferior coal that contains clay or other fine-grained mineral matter, must be removed from the quality coal to insure a better product. The process for picking or separating bone was performed by hand outside the mine, and the miner was paid less money for picking coal than he was for entering the mines to dig for it. Dad, anxious to earn more money so our family could have a place of our own, gave up the safe, but less lucrative, job of picking bone to move inside the mines. Seven days a week, he loaded coal from the belly of the mountain, earning sixty-five cents for every five tons of coal he dug. The coal company allowed miners to work as many hours a week as they could tolerate, so Dad took advantage of the overtime work. My parents were a great team. Not only was Dad a hard worker, but my mother was a prudent money manager, and it wasn't too long before their savings began to grow right along with the family. In January 1916, Adamo Andrea, their second son (affectionately nicknamed Di) was born.

Working in the mines was not an easy life, as it was hard, dirty, and dangerous. Accidents happened often in the little community, and tragedy eventually struck our family. My Uncle Carl and Uncle Joe, who were in their early thirties, were killed in separate mining accidents only months apart. Needless to say, it was devastating for the family. Even before their deaths, Dad had been very concerned about the growing number of mine accidents happening at the American Coal Mine. Dad, who was superstitious (as were most immigrants), believed the deaths were omens, and he told my mother, "If I stay, I will die." My parents approached the Cameresis about Dad's concerns, and after much discussion, my parents made the decision to move. Two months after Joe's funeral, we said our tearful good-byes to the Cameresi family.

Dad, who spoke very little English and had no formal training, had very few wage-earning options. Although it was dangerous work, his only opportunity to earn significant money was in the coal mining industry, but which one should he choose? Although there were a number of coal camps located near McComas, Dad decided to move our family to another county and chose Trailee Coal Camp, located outside Mullens, West Virginia. We traveled by horse and buggy, which was loaded with our sparse belongings, to the train station in Princeton, West Virginia. We boarded the train and began a winding ride through the mountains. Four hours later, we arrived at our destination.

Unlike today, Mullens was a bustling little town during the early 1900s. The base population was around two thousand, but Mullens attracted a large number of folks who lived in the surrounding area. It was a progressive town that offered a variety of shopping and entertainment. There were several locally owned grocery stores, numerous restaurants, three hotels, two movie theaters, a Coca-Cola plant, dress shops, jewelry stores, a Murphy's five-and-dime store complete with a large lunch counter, and two drugstores. All were frame buildings, and some were two-storied. Three passenger trains arrived daily, bringing salesmen, visitors, and shoppers to town.

There was a privately owned toll bridge at the south end of town. The toll was five cents per person for those who walked and ten cents for a horse and buggy. When the water was low, people who did not pay the toll forded the river beneath the bridge where the Slab Fork and Guyandotte Rivers joined.

I am not sure when they paved the roads, but I vividly remember the muddy streets that had to be navigated when it rained. Rocks and boards served as sidewalks, so people could avoid the mud. The main sources of the local economy that brought people to town were the seventeen coal mines and the Norfolk Railroad electric shops located in areas near the town.

Being six years old, I was inquisitive, but I did not question Dad's move. I have regretted many times that I did not ask him why he chose Mullens when there were other towns we could have lived in that were closer to McComas. It could be that Dad was aware of the prosperity in Mullens. All I do know for certain is his decision to settle near Mullens set the foundation for my blessed life.

When we arrived in our new town, Dad began working in the Trailee Coal Mines, and we rented a small house at the Trailee Coal Camp. The coal camp, located on the outskirts of town, was similar to the McComas coal camp, with rows of small, company-owned houses, but I don't think there were any coke ovens. Dad returned to work in the mines, with my parents still focused on their goal. While living at Trailee, Olga, my sister and my parent's third child, was born.

In 1919, not too long after we had moved, my parents' dream to own a business was realized. Dad opened his first store in Mullens and proudly named it D'Antoni's Grocery Store. Located across the street from the railroad station, it was a two-story gray frame building with two large picture windows and the name "D'Antoni's" boldly written in script across the top of each window. The store was both a business and our home, as we lived on the second story of the building. Our new home was very small, with only a living room and two small bedrooms. Di and I shared one bedroom, while Olga, still a baby, slept in a bassinette in my parents' bedroom. The kitchen was located on the first floor, adjacent to the main area of the grocery store.

I can still visualize my dad standing proudly in front of the store that displayed his name. On more than one occasion, he reminded me that honoring the name D'Antoni was the only thing he expected. And I repeated it to my children since the time they could comprehend the importance of the message.

My father's large clientele included folks in town, who he offered the courtesy of delivering groceries by horse and buggy, and the visitors who arrived daily by train, who bought lunches and sundries from him. In the summers, I occasionally worked for my dad selling ice cream. A clever businessman, he directed me to strategically locate my ice cream stand near the railroad station so the daily visitors could become customers as soon as they stepped off the train and eyed the delicious treat. It is interesting to me that a number of articles or books detail how children living in the early 1900s worked in the fields from sunup to sundown. My recollection of childhood is totally different. Although I had an ice cream sales job and did a few odd jobs for my father, mostly I played. I didn't have regular household or work chores, much to the chagrin of my mother. Dad, whose youth was spent working long hours under the abusive hand of his own father, rarely assigned me chores. My youth was spent enjoying the status of a firstborn son in an Italian family who chose America as their home.

The one chore my father requested of me involved wine. Wine making, an age-old Italian tradition, was lovingly practiced in our home. Wine was a daily staple, and on many mornings, breakfast consisted of wine poured over a thick slice of homemade bread that had been sprinkled with sugar. Rather than buying wine for the family, Dad enjoyed making his own. This was legal as long as it was used for personal consumption and not for sale.

Each year, Dad ordered a large shipment of grapes from New York. Part of the shipment was sold in his store, and the rest went to making homemade wine. Everyone was involved in the annual winemaking at our home, and Dad expected me to play a role in the distilling process. A large wooden tub, set up in our basement, was filled with imported plump, ripe grapes. My job was to crush the grapes into a thick mush. After school, I would go to the basement, wash my feet, and climb into the large tub to stomp the grapes. After a couple of hours, the grapes would be the right consistency, and Dad would place them in a large burlap sack that he hung over a big barrel. Over time, the juice from the grapes slowly dripped through the sack into the large barrel, eventually fermenting. After the fermenting process was complete, Dad bottled the wine.

My strongest memory of wine making was not the process, but what resulted from stomping the grapes. The juice from the grapes stained my feet a very dark purple color, which lasted a couple of weeks. Taking showers after ball practice or ball games with my teammates proved to be quite tedious and embarrassing. My purple feet were the butt of many jokes and the cause of raucous laughter in the locker room. Being shy, I offered no verbal response to their taunts in the locker room, but enjoyed answering them with my actions on the playing field. To use a cliché, these actions were much louder than words.

In the spring of 1920, I was playing marbles with friends in the alley behind our store. Nearby was a dry cleaning plant that used gasoline in its cleaning process. My friends and I were in the middle of a serious marble game when a loud explosion rang out. Looking up, we saw a guy covered in flames running out of the building. Within seconds, the entire dry cleaning plant was swallowed in fire. The flames, which were spreading quickly to the adjacent buildings, headed straight for Dad's store and our home. Frightened, I ran to our store as fast as I could. I knew Dad was delivering groceries and my mother and little sister were home alone. Hollering, "Fire! Fire!" as loudly as I could, I ran upstairs looking for my mother. I grabbed my baby sister from the crib while Mom gathered as many of our things as she could. The flames rose higher and higher as the frame buildings fueled the hungry fire. We fled the house, running to a safe area near the train station. Di, who was playing down the street when the fire broke out, spotted us coming out of the building and ran to join us. In a few short minutes, the fire claimed D'Antoni's. We watched in horror as our store and home burned to the ground. Everything was gone. What had taken years to achieve was destroyed in less than thirty minutes.

Dad returned home to find his dream vanished. He stood frozen in total disbelief. Scanning the ashes of his property, he saw a piece of broken glass partially bearing the name "D'Antoni's" protruding from the smoldering ashes. He did not see his family. Anxiously searching the area and peering through the thick smoke that was rising from the rubble, Dad sighed in relief as he found his family silently waiting for him on the small grassy knoll in front of the train station. He ran to us. After giving us much-needed consoling hugs and checking to see if everyone was okay, Dad surveyed the damage. Finally, he gathered his family and, with quiet determination, began the process of rebuilding our lives. Just as the broken glass bearing the name "D'Antoni" was rising out of the ashes, he too would successfully climb back and get past this horrific obstacle. Watching my dad courageously handle this tragic moment with total calm and dignity taught me a great lesson in resiliency and tenacity, one that I have used during difficult times in my life.

Andrea and Fiordoliva Cameresi D'Antoni

**(seated left to right) Anna, Olga (standing
left to right) Adamo (Di), Luigi**

After the fire, we moved to Nuriva, a small coal camp
located near Mullens. Dad returned to work in the mines with
one goal in mind: rebuilding his store and home. He worked
long, hard hours mining coal and did not miss a day of work for

an entire year. After that one year was up, he and my mother had saved enough money to not only rebuild our grocery store in downtown Mullens, but to purchase a residential lot, lot 12, on Moran Avenue. Within sixteen months of the fire, D'Antoni's Grocery Store was back in business, and construction on our new home was underway.

Our family moved from the small house in the coal camp to the second story of the rebuilt store. In 1924, Anna, my second sister, was born. We lived in the small living space over the store until 1928, when we moved to our new two-story brick home on Moran Avenue. The new house came with all the conveniences of the time: a daily delivery of milk to our doorstep, a large coal furnace complete with a coal shoot in the basement window of the house, a kitchen equipped with a large icebox (which actually held a large block of ice), and a crank-style telephone. Our new telephone system offered two types of service: a party line, which served multiple families, and a private line, which was limited to one family. Both services connected us to our neighbors and friends in other towns and were managed by local operators. Regardless of the type of line in use, the telephone operators placed each call, and they knew (and shared) more about folks in town than the local newspaper. Until 1976, our telephone number was 546. Life was good.

After years of hard work peppered with heartache and misfortune, Andrea and Flora had again realized their dream. They owned a successful business, and they had a large family and a wonderful home. At ninety-five, I still choose to live in that same brick home on Moran Avenue.

A year after we moved into our new home, my mother became gravely ill. Dad sought medical help everywhere, including a trip to Johns Hopkins Hospital in Maryland. But, it was to no avail; no one could help my mother. Fiordoliva Cameresi D'Antoni died of kidney failure on Saturday, June 2, 1929, at St. Luke's Hospital in Princeton, West Virginia. Mom was only thirty-six years old. Dad was widowed with four children to raise—me, age sixteen; Adamo Andrea, age thirteen; Olga, age eight; and Anna, age five. Once again, as I watched the pain cut deeply into my father's heart and into our family, he quietly and courageously gathered himself together in the face of adversity and, without a word of complaint, moved forward with our lives.

Trouble next struck my dad only four months after my mothers' death when the Bank of Mullens failed. The ugly reality of the stock market crash reached all the way to our small community in West Virginia, and my dad lost most of his money. Depositors at the bank received ten cents on the dollar, but once again, Dad accepted the reality and countered by working longer hours. Later, I discovered Dad actually blamed the failure of the bank personally on the three men who owned the bank. The policies of his new country, which he dearly loved, could not be the blame, and his zeal to recover his losses was driven, in part, by his determination to prove to the bank owners that he would and could survive. And he did.

Grocery store chains began to move into Mullens in the mid 1930s, and Dad could not compete with their low prices. Understanding the situation, he remodeled the grocery store and turned it into a beer garden. The beer garden flourished, and soon business was booming, providing Dad with more than adequate earnings. His young family was also flourishing, and we had many friends in Mullens who played a positive role in our lives. My grandparents, Speranza and Luigi Camersi, came to live with us for about a year and helped with the children. The Kirbys, our next door neighbors, also reached out to us, and we were always welcome to eat breakfast at their house before we left for school. The town was filled with wonderful people who always were willing to help their neighbors. The camaraderie that existed (and still exists) there is the backbone of the numerous success stories that are now part of Mullens's history.

Later in Dad's life, when all of his children were grown and on their own, he married Rosie Rezzonico. Their union created an even larger D'Antoni family, as Bruna, Bill, and Louie, Rosie's three wonderful children, became part of our family.

My memories of my dad are very strong. I have so much respect for him and his commitment to succeed. He was incredible. Today, people discuss all their challenges, but in my opinion, they have none. After coming to a new country with no family; not knowing the language; having no education; losing his business, his home, and his wife; raising four children alone; and suffering a devastating financial loss, he not only survived, he thrived. And, through all the hardship, I never once heard my dad utter one word of complaint. His actions taught me a lesson that has served me well throughout my personal and professional life. A person's fate is determined by how he chooses to react to adversity. It is easy to be a winner. The mark of a man or a team is the ability to withstand misfortune, to learn from it, to set the bad results aside, and to implement a strategy for success.

Chapter Four:

Childhood

As hard as my father worked, he did not require or expect the same hard work from his children. He believed they should have the freedom to enjoy their childhood, so, as a youngster, my time was spent playing games, going to the movies, and fishing in the clear, deep Guyandotte River that ran along the side of the town. I was pretty much on my own.

One game I enjoyed was shinny, a game played with tin cans and a stick. It was named "shinny" because your shins were bruised by the end of play. Run-sheepy-run, a forerunner to the game of tag, was another game of choice. But the game that we spent the most hours playing was marbles.

Saturday was the best day of the week because that was the day marbles contests were held in Mullens. Players from around the area would arrive in town by train. Each boy would be toting a bag of marbles and looking for friendly competition. Some days, there may have been fifty or more players who began playing by 8:00 AM and didn't stop until dark. The marbles game of keeps was the usual game of choice. In keeps, the players would first agree upon the number of marbles placed in the middle of a large circle, which was called the ring. The object was to shoot at the marbles, knocking them out of the circle. The taw marble, which was the shooting marble, was slightly bigger than the other ones. As long as the participant continued to knock marbles out of the ring but leave the taw marble inside, he held his turn. All the marbles knocked out of the ring by the shooter became the shooter's property, thus the name "keeps." Once the shooter failed to hit a marble out of the ring, another player took his turn. Not to brag, but I had amassed a real nice collection of marbles.

We played with a variety of agates, the shooting marbles. Two of my favorites were moonies and steelies. The moonie had a unique characteristic. Every time the moonie hit another marble, a small moon shape appeared on its surface. The more successes a player had, the more moonies appeared on the marble's surface. It was fascinating to see. The steelie was a small marble made of solid steel. In competition, all players had to agree to a steelie being used because it was a heavier marble. Some players thought it gave the user an unfair advantage.

Rolley hole was another popular marble game. The rolley hole court consisted of three or four shallow holes that were dug in a straight line, ten to fifteen feet apart. The last hole, which was very small, was called the peewee hole. The starting line for the game was approximately three feet back from the first hole. The object of the game was to shoot a marble into all the holes. The winner was the first person to shoot his marble into the peewee hole. The winner kept all the marbles in the game or the game was played for knucks. To play for knucks meant whoever lost the game was required to put his knuckles down and over one side of the first hole. The winner positioned himself on the other side of the hole and was entitled to shoot his marble at the loser's knuckles. The number of times the winner shot at the loser's knuckles was determined before the game started. If more than two players were in the game, the last person who finished endured everyone else shooting at him. I can tell you from experience: you didn't want to lose. Knucks may just have been the game that molded my compelling desire to win. It definitely made a lasting impression—on my mind and my knuckles.

My love for marbles as a kid was common knowledge in local sports lore, and during my coaching days in Mullens, George Springer, a sports writer for a West Virginia newspaper, asked me to set up an annual marble tournament in Mullens. I agreed. The playing surface for the marble tournament was a huge roll of linoleum that covered the cafeteria floor at Mullens High School. Each year, hundreds of kids from the local communities would vie for the marble champion crown. The tournament was very popular, and one year, George invited me to take a group of marble players to the national championship in Wildwood, New Jersey. Again, I agreed. In addition to the national marble competition for youngsters, there was a chaperone's marble tournament, which I decided to enter. That year, we came home to Mullens victorious with two championships. One was the national marble champion, Pee Wee Bowers, and the other was the chaperone marble champion, me. Unfortunately, over the years, the sport of marbles has died.

If I wasn't playing marbles as a kid, then I might be found fishing. Di and I spent a lot of time setting trotlines on the rough Guyan, located between Mullens and Pineville. A trotline was a long wire that had fishing hooks tied to it. The wire stretched across the river and was anchored to a tree on each river bank. We would bait the hooks with helgamites or night crawlers and then wait. The next morning, we would swim the trot line and bag the fish.

Most of the fish we caught were mud cats, channel cats, bass, and occasionally redhorses (suckers). At other times, where the river was not so deep, Bud Hypes, a good friend of mine, would join Di and me for "snag" fishing. We would tie three hooks together to make an effective snare device. Taking this homemade device, we would wade out into the clear river, lower the fishing snare into the water, and stand quietly waiting for the fish to swim by us. As the fish swam by our legs, we

My Prize Catfish Catch

would sense the right moment and jerk the line in an upward motion, snagging the fish.

At least once a week, I left marble playing and fishing behind and went to a movie. Going to the movies was a special treat for Di and me, and the ones I remembered most were about cowboys. Movies were black and white and silent back then. The only way people could follow the story was by reading the captions printed on the screen. In the background, there was live organ music, which set the mood on the screen, whether happy, sad, funny, exciting, or dangerous. Eventually, sound made its way into the movies, and we watched excitedly as the cowboys came alive on the screen. Dad was a huge fan of the cowboy movies, and occasionally, he would leave his business to attend. He would get so engaged in the action that he would talk excitedly to the characters on the screen, warning the good guys as to the whereabouts of the bad guys. "Watch out, they're behind the rocks," he would shout. Nobody would seem to notice my dad's outbursts, as everyone was the same as Dad, totally engrossed in what was happening on the screen.

Chapter Five:

Baseball—Babe Ruth and Gats

In the 1920s, there were no community or playground basketball courts in Mullens. Like most small towns in America, the only basketball courts were located in schools and were regulated by the local school system. So, football, which required no court, was my favorite pastime, until Dad came home one evening with a present for me. It was a brand new baseball glove. Over the next few years, the glove became a natural extension of my arm, as I rarely took it off. It was my first love affair; I fell completely under the spell of baseball. Organized high school baseball did not exist during this time, but Mullens had a good semipro baseball team. It was a thrill to attend their practices, and I became a regular groupie, always hanging around during batting practices. My consistent presence at the team's practices paid big dividends. When I was fourteen, the manager allowed me to go into the outfield during batting practices and shag balls. As a result, catching fly balls became second nature to me.

My love of baseball was the reason for my first trip out of Mullens without adult supervision. I was sixteen years old, and Dad gave me permission to go with a group of friends to a baseball game in Washington, DC. Joe Santon, a man from Mullens, worked at the Washington Senators' ballpark. He called one day to tell me that the Yankees were on the schedule for the next game against the Senators and asked if I wanted to bring some guys and come to the game—we could get in free. Wow! Wanted to come? Who wouldn't jump at the chance to see Babe Ruth, Lou Gehrig, Tony Lassari, and Earl Combs? Without hesitation, I took Joe up on his offer and had no trouble finding a group of guys who wanted to go on the trip. All of us were fifteen or sixteen and still in high school, except for Mac Shumate, who we asked to go because he was over eighteen and had a driver's license. At that time, eighteen was the required age for a license. After we found a driver, we were faced with one last problem. We had to find a car. Oscar England, a friend of my dad, heard about our problem and offered to let us use his touring car. The car, which had a number of years on it, did not have good tires, but it seated six people and filled our need. Thanking Oscar, we took him up on his offer. So, on a sunny Saturday morning in June, we took off for Washington, DC.

We had barely driven three miles out of town when Mac pulled the car off the road and addressed the group. "Okay guys, I have to tell you this before we go any further."

"Now what's the problem, Mac?" I asked.

"Well, we all agreed we would take enough money to pay our own way, but I got to tell you guys, I don't have any money."

I didn't doubt him, as these were the depression years, and unlike the rest of us who were still in high school, Mac was going from one job to another trying to make ends meet. We didn't have much money either, just what our parents had given us, but we realized it didn't matter if Mac had money or not—he was the only one with a driver's license. If we were going to the game, Mac was going to the game. After a few minutes of counting our money, we agreed to pay Mac's way. With the bargain struck, we headed to Washington, D.C.

The trip was eventful, taking longer than usual because the car was well worn. After patching several flat tires along the way, we finally arrived at Washington's ballpark. Joe kept his word and got us into the game. What a day! A day I will never forget. Not only did Babe Ruth hit a homerun and Lou Gehrig have several hits, we watched a close thriller with the beloved Yankees winning.

Sitting in our seats after the game talking about all we had seen, it was obvious we were bitten by the baseball bug and definitely not ready to go home. It was just too much fun; we had to see more. Knowing the Yankees were playing the next day in Philadelphia, we counted our money and came to the conclusion that we had enough to continue to Philadelphia to see the next game. We spent the night, six of us in one room, at a cheap hotel in D.C. The next morning, we left for Philadelphia. By the time we got to the ballpark, it had started to rain. The ticket master at the stadium told us the game was rained out but if we wanted to see the Yankees in action, they were playing in New York the next day. Disappointed, but determined to see more of Ruth and company, we decided to catch the game in New York. After all, we were already almost there.

On our way out of Philadelphia, we came to a stop at a red light. Instead of waiting for the light to turn green, Mac, for some unknown reason, took a sudden right turn down a side street and then abruptly crossed over to another street. Not too long after that, we heard police sirens in the distance. Someone made the comment, "Gosh, somebody's in big trouble." The sirens got louder and louder. Suddenly, two motorcycle cops pulled in front of our car, two pulled in behind, and one alongside the car. All motioned for us to pull over. We were scared to death. We had never been outside the city limits of Mullens by ourselves and weren't sure what was happening. All we knew was that we were in big trouble. The police ordered us out of the car and began searching it. After not finding anything, they began questioning us individually. One policeman took my arm and walked me away from the group. He asked, "Where are you from?"

I answered, "Mullens, West Virginia."

He looked me over. "What are you doing up here?" he demanded.

Nervously, I replied, "Well, we wanted to see some ball games. We saw the Senators play the Yankees and decided to come to Philadelphia to see another game here. It was rained out, so we are on our way to a game in New York."

Skeptical of my answer he barked, "How much money you got?"

Pulling my money out of my pocket, I answered, "I've got around $20."

The policeman stared at me. "Isn't that a lot of money for you to have?" he finally questioned.

"No," I said. "Going on a trip like this, you have to have money."

He continued to stare at me. Finally, he demanded, "Where's your gat?"

"Gat? What's a gat?" I had no idea what he meant.

He looked at me like I was either lying or stupid. "You know, a revolver, a pistol," he said.

Horrified, I quickly responded, "I don't have any gun or pistol."

"Are you sure?" he asked as he patted me down. Finally satisfied that I didn't have a gun on me, he took me back to where the others were waiting.

Mac, who was notoriously outspoken, started to argue with the officers. I told him to shut up before he got us in more trouble. Still unconvinced we were innocent, the police told us to get back in the car, and they escorted us to the police station. At the station, they herded us into a small holding area. I have to admit, we did look like a bunch of bums. We hadn't shaved in two days and had slept in our clothes the night before. After making us wait, they began to question us again. "Okay, now where did you say you were from?"

I spoke up and said, "Mullens, West Virginia Why don't you call the state trooper there? His name is Trooper Platt. He can vouch for us."

Thinking it over, the policeman finally agreed, so I followed him into the next office where he called Platt. When he answered the phone, the Philadelphia policeman told him he had six guys in custody who claimed to be from Mullens and he was calling to verify their statements. He read off our names. After listening to all the names being read, Platt waited a moment, and then I could hear him quip, "I don't know anybody by those names. Put their asses in jail."

The policeman turned to me and stated, "He said he doesn't know who you are. He told me to put your ass in jail."

Panicking, I said, "Let me have that phone. Let me talk to him."

Grabbing the phone from the policeman, I yelled into the phone, "Platt, damn you, you better tell them who we are. This isn't funny; they're going to throw us in jail."

After a deep chuckle, Platt remarked, "Oh, hell, D'Antoni, I was just having a little fun. Put the guy back on the line." Platt finally verified our story, and the Philadelphia police released us. Before we left, they told us that earlier that afternoon in Camden, New Jersey, six guys in a touring car with an out-of-state license plate held up a bank and killed a policeman. When we made the right turn at the red light, our car caught their attention and they thought we were the culprits. Standing on the steps of the police station with our freedom restored, we decided the Yankees game didn't have the same appeal any-more. We had had enough big-city living to last us a lifetime, so we started our journey back home.

When we arrived in New Market, Virginia, our car tire blew. It had been repaired so many times that it couldn't be patched. If we were going to get back to Mullens in the car, we were going to have to replace the tire. The problem was that we had very little money. As our car limped into a filling station, I was elected as the spokesperson to explain our troubles to the station owner. After checking out the cost of a tire, I explained to the owner we were quite a ways from our destination and didn't have a lot of money. He didn't seem very sympathetic, so I said, "I've got this wrist watch. Would you take it for money?" He inspected the watch and agreed to the trade. Searching in the remote corners of his station, he found a well-used tire and gave it to me. Replacing the tire, we continued on our way.

We were finally back in West Virginia and about two hours from home in a small town called Hinton when the car abruptly stopped. It was obvious that it was not going any further. We pushed it off of the main highway and into a man's front yard. Knocking on the front door of the house, we explained to the home owner about our car trouble and asked if it would be okay to leave the car in his yard until someone from Mullens could tow it. Luckily, he agreed.

Worn out and anxious to get home, we began hitchhiking. Not too far down the road, a truck that was carrying chickens stopped. A farmer stuck his head out of the driver's side of the truck and commented, "You boys can ride with me if you don't mind riding in back with the chickens." Happily, we climbed aboard. So what if chicken feathers were flying everywhere? We were tired, we weren't walking, and home was not far away. Traveling toward Mullens, a final obstacle, a toll bridge, came into view. After the driver stopped the truck, he turned around and asked us for sixty cents—ten cents per person for the toll. Somehow, we managed to scrape up the money to get across the bridge. The next stop was in Beckley, a town about twenty miles from Mullens, and the farmer's destination. He stopped at a local filling station, and we jumped off the back of the truck. After brushing the chicken feathers off my clothes and hair, I went inside and called Dad. He sent someone to pick us up. Never in my life have I been as happy to see the city-limits sign for Mullens, West Virginia. What an adventure. Some time would pass before I considered another trip out of town. That night, I dreamed of Babe Ruth's homerun and gats.

It is interesting that as adults, all of us have chosen to live in small towns instead of in cities. I wonder if our big-city adventure influenced our decision.

Chapter Six:

Superstition and Prejudice

Two illogical facts of life—superstition and prejudice—subconsciously impact the way people treat each other, and for my generation, they were major components of life. Dad, who was very superstitious, not only believed in his dreams, he interpreted them himself. Needless to say, at times his dreams influenced his decision making. Betty Jo, who was fearless to a fault, had won Dad's heart quickly and came face-to-face early in our marriage with the perils of Dad's superstitions.

As stated previously, fourteen years after my mother's death, Dad married Rosie Rezzonico, a widow who lived in Mullens. Living nearby was Columbia, my mother's niece, who was crippled from birth. She lived with her parents on top of a mountain about eight miles outside of Mullens. One of Dad's superstition was the belief that physically handicapped people were endowed with special powers and were capable of putting the "*l'occhi*," the Italian word for hexes, on another person.

Shortly after his marriage to Rosie, Dad's left leg started to bother him. Having never been sick a day in his life, he began to suspect foul play. He came to the conclusion that the pain in his leg was the result of a hex that Columbia had placed on him for marrying another woman.

Early one snowy morning, Dad marched into our home and instructed Betty Jo to call a cab. He announced that he was going to his niece's house to take care of a hex that she had put on him. I wasn't home at the time, so Betty Jo, alarmed by Dad's determination, decided to take matters into her own hands. She told Dad there was no need for a cab, and that she would drive him to Columbia's house. As they slowly made their way up the snowy mountain road, Betty Jo tried to convince Dad that his pain was not a hex. Her explanations fell on deaf ears. Dad had made up his mind.

Heavy footsteps and sharp knocking on Columbia's front door announced their arrival. Surprised, but happy to see them, Columbia's mother invited them inside. Totally obsessed with his mission, Dad stormed past her and demanded to see Columbia. As Columbia wheeled into the room, Dad began bellowing in Italian, accusing her of witchcraft and evil spells. Columbia, visibly shaken as Dad's Italian rage intensified, was speechless. Betty Jo, concerned by what was taking place, quickly stated, "Columbia, take the hex off of Mr. Dan now and we'll leave!" Winking at the frightened girl, she hoped Columbia would understand and go along with the idea. Nervous, but following Betty Jo's lead, Columbia looked at Dad and stated she would remove the hex. Dad hesitated for a moment. Gathering courage from the silence, Columbia regained her composure and emphatically assured him the hex was removed. Dad continued to stare at Columbia and then suddenly, without a word, turned and marched out the door. With an apologetic gesture, Betty Jo followed.

As Dad approached the car, he slipped on the snow. A small handgun fell out of his pocket. Taken aback by the sudden awareness of his initial intent, Betty Jo whispered a grateful prayer. Heavy silence hung over the drive home until Dad looked at Betty Jo and, with a thick Italian accent, flatly remarked, "I me leg don't hurta no more!" Evidently, the l'occhi had been successfully removed.

Along with superstition, prejudice during this time period was also prevalent, and I learned quickly that there were people who felt superior to me because of my name, D'Antoni. Crude remarks, whispers behind my back, banishments from certain collegiate social clubs, and being unwelcome in many places were part of my social reality growing up.

It was a difficult period for me. I was sixteen years old, a sophomore in high school, and my mom had died. I watched my dad, sadly, but with great resolve, refocus his life. Mom's illness created a financial strain for Dad, and as a result, he worked longer hours at his business. I think this helped allow him time to grieve privately and it helped him provide financial security for his children. I coped by immersing myself into sports. Not only did it occupy my time and thoughts, it provided a haven for me against prejudice.

Sports were the only sanctuary that offered me a level playing field. They were an opportunity to prove what a D'Antoni could do, and in so doing, I was considered an equal. I was determined to be as good as or even better than my teammates, the "American" kids.

Thankfully, this was not a common occurrence in Mullens, as most of the townspeople embraced my family and helped Dad rebuild his life. My experiences with prejudice happened mainly outside the city limits. Even though prejudice reared its ugly head during my childhood, the upside was the positive outcomes it played in my development as a person. I became mentally stronger, grew more resilient, and developed a strong determination to succeed.

Betty Jo and I were keenly aware of the ugliness that comes from prejudice, and we knew, like the old adage states, that prejudice is very carefully taught. We were determined that this behavior would never exist in our home. Once more, Betty Jo accepted the challenge, and two humorous incidents on how she countered prejudice are part of my memories.

Not long after we were married, Betty Jo and her sister attended an out-of-town football game that I was coaching. It was my first coaching job at Mullens High School. The bleachers were packed with fans. Sitting directly behind Betty Jo was a raucous group of men who had been "nipping" to stave off the cool autumn night. It was a close game, and the group of men questioned my substitution patterns and my ability to call the right plays. The critics' comments were loud enough for Betty Jo to overhear, but she chose to ignore them. The complaints grew louder and louder until suddenly one man shouted over the crowd noise, "Who picked you as coach? Who decided Mullens should hire a 'tally coach? You need to go back where you came from, wop!"

That did it! Betty Jo jumped out of her seat, whirled around, and with a look that could have killed the man where he sat, she demanded, "And just what boat did your ancestors come over on? The boat with all the murderers and thieves, or the one with all the whores?"

The man was speechless. Betty Jo, satisfied, smiled sweetly at the crowd that had turned to watch the confrontation, sat back down in her seat, and finished watching the game. By the way, the new 'tally coach won the ball game.

The second incident involved Betty Jo and our two boys, Mike, who was six years old at the time, and Danny, who was eleven. They were on a road trip to Maryland to pick up Kathy, our daughter. On the way back to Mullens, they decided to stop for lunch. Betty Jo was confident that she knew how to pick out good restaurants. Her theory was if there were a lot of cars in the restaurant's parking lot, then it was a sign they served good food, no matter what the building looked like. It was nearing lunchtime, and Betty Jo had everyone on the lookout for a place to eat. They were about to pass a small run-down roadside restaurant when she noticed a large number of cars in the parking lot. Betty Jo slowed the car and pulled into the lot, knowing she had found the right place. Entering the restaurant, it became apparent it was a local hangout for the Mexican field laborers in the area. As the small D'Antoni entourage walked toward a table, the talking abruptly stopped.

All eyes turned, scrutinizing the newcomers. Danny, who was the self-appointed family protector for the trip, whispered to the group, "We better get out of here. This place is full of Mexicans!"

Betty Jo calmly but firmly grabbed Danny's shirt sleeve, pulled him into a seat at a table, and with authority quietly stated, "Sit down, you little 'tally. We're having lunch." Our children got the message loud and clear.

Chapter Seven:

Team Sports 1920s–1930s

My athletic skills may be the result of all the games I played as a child. I think my quickness can be attributed to the daily route I walked to school. After our home was destroyed by fire, we moved outside the Mullens city limits. I walked two-and-a-half miles (not ten) to school every day, unless I took the shortcut, which was not for the faint of heart. It was through a train tunnel that was one hundred yards long, which is the length of a football field. The tunnel was very busy, as local trains made dozens of trips daily. But, for a ten-year-old with the guts to enter the large black hole, the shortcut took almost a mile off the walk. Every day, I opted for the shortcut, and my routine for dealing with the tunnel never varied. Near the opening of the tunnel, I would stop, take a deep breath, and visualize standing on the starting line for the hundred-yard dash. When the gun went off in my head, I ran through the tunnel. Thank goodness I always won the race. The experience was great practice for my future football days.

In 1928, I entered the eighth grade, which was the first year of high school. There were no junior varsity teams. My freshman year was the first year I was allowed to practice with the varsity teams, but I wasn't allowed to play in regulation games. In the tenth grade, I was a starter on the football and basketball teams. Unfortunately, my dad did not come to many games because he was usually working. But I was always keenly aware of his support and the pride he felt when our team won.

I feel the same fatherly pride when I walk into Madison Square Garden to watch my son Mike's team, the New York Knicks, play. I had the same tingling nerves, excitement, and anticipation every time I walked into a packed high school gym in 1930. If I close my eyes and concentrate, I can hear the sounds echoing from my past: the screeching of tennis shoes, the thump of the balls, the shrill whistles, and the spectator noise. There are also memories of the uniforms, the basketball, and the gyms as how they interplay with today's world.

My basketball uniform consisted of short shorts, black high-top Converse tennis shoes, and a jersey made of material that scratched the body. The jersey was made out of wool, and anyone who plays or has played competitive basketball knows how uncomfortable these jerseys become just ten minutes into a ball game. Thank goodness that by the time I got to college, the material for the jersey had changed to a heavy nylon. As for the basketball shorts, instead of progressing in styles, they have regressed. I never dreamed basketball shorts would become baggy and as long as bloomers from the 1920s.

The basketball, which was very heavy, had a bladder, a stem, and laces that tied it together. Dribbling the ball required concentration and the ability to correct the bounce in a minute's notice if it hit on one of the laces at an odd angle. As you might surmise, passes were the play of choice for moving the ball up the floor.

The most intriguing change in basketball has been the evolution of the gymnasium. Today, high school and college basketball gyms are functional pieces of beautiful art. Some basketball complexes I have visited are almost breathtaking in their design. Included within the complexes are major workout and training facilities, plush seating for spectators, sky

My High School Basketball Picture (notice the "wine" stained hands)

boxes for the financial elite, and concession stands offering top-notch cuisine during the game. In comparison to the gyms where I played or coached basketball, the changes that have occurred are incredible.

In the early years, basketball gymnasiums had no specification regarding size or requirements. It wasn't until the '50s that it became important to standardize facilities. Prior to that, there was no regulation on size, seating, or design, and consequently gyms differed greatly from school to school. Some schools had only outdoor courts available for games.

Poised and Ready for Hoop Action

Mullens High School's gym, which was one of the smallest in the area, was built in 1928 and doubled as the school's auditorium. The floor was seventy feet by thirty feet, and one end had a stage with a roll-down basket that was attached to the ceiling. Padded mats were placed on the apron of the stage to prevent injuries. The homemade scoreboard was located on the stage, and the scorekeeper turned the numbers by hand.

For spectator seating, a set of bleachers was located on the opposite end. When ball games were played, metal chairs were set up along the edge of the out-of-bounds line encircling the floor to accommodate additional spectators. The fortunate fans were the ones who arrived early to get a seat, as others had to stand behind the metal chairs, where there was enough room to accommodate fans standing three-deep. Filled to capacity, the gym held three hundred spectators.

Each gym in the area where I played had its own personality. Oceana High School, one of our county rivals, had a large gym but very little seating space. In each corner of the gym stood a large Bunsen wood-burning stove to heat the gym. No locker rooms or showers were available, so we dressed in a classroom that was located in a separate building. To get to the gym, we had to go outside between buildings, and on snowy or rainy nights, it was always a cold, wet trek to the gym.

Another county gym that gave me and my team a different challenge was located in Baileysville. The gym's ceiling was so low that we could not use a lob pass. Supporting the ceiling were four large wood poles running floor to ceiling. One pole was located at each end of the foul line on both ends of the floor. During the game, each team seemed to have two extra players on the floor because the wooden poles acted as stationary players who provided wonderful picks.

Maben High School, located in the northern end of the county, had a very unique gym. The court was surrounded by very little floor space. Only one side of the gym had barely enough room for the team benches and a few spectators. Under the goals, there may have been two feet of space in front of the wall. It was so cramped that the out-of-bounds line for the side of the court opposite the team benches was a thick red line located on the wall. The line was drawn about three feet up from the floor and ran the length of the floor, continuing behind both baskets. If the ball hit below the line, it was still in play, and if the ball hit the wall above the red line, it was ruled out of bounds.

Many of the gyms we played in had their own idiosyncrasies, but the Hinton Gym was the most distinctive. It was a shot-altering gym. Eight feet above both foul lines, spanning the width of the floor, was a large I beam that supported the roof. To score a basket beyond the foul line, the shooter had to arch the ball over the I beam to get the shot to the basket. Playing in this gym required unusual basketball skills.

As a matter of fact, when coaches laid out a game plan, the gym layout was a major factor, and the plan was tailored for each facility. Using the physical structure to an advantage, the coaches added additional dimensions to their ability to design game strategies. This is one interesting aspect of yesteryear's game that today's coach does not have to address.

Recently, as I sat waiting on a Knicks game to begin and watching the teams warm up for the game, I noticed the athletic trainers working with the players by stretching them out and putting them through special exercises. Over in a corner sat a stationary bicycle that was used to keep hamstring muscles from tightening up. I chuckled to myself as I remembered the required conditioning for sports in my day, especially in football.

During my playing days, conditioning as we know it today was never considered. Just showing up for practice meant you met the requirements for being ready and able to play. Lifting weights, stretching, and proper nourishment were not part of the program. Hydrating the body before and during competition is highly recommended for athletes today. I never drank water during a game or a practice. It was thought that drinking too much water caused a player to be waterlogged and not able to move quickly.

During my school days, the football uniform design was quite different from what is worn today. My football helmet was made of soft, flimsy leather, and at the end of a game, I would fold my helmet up and carry it in the back pocket of my pants. The pants hip and knee pads were actually sewn into the pants, and rib pants didn't exist. Football jerseys, which were very heavy and made from wool, were extremely hot. Our shoes, which were equipped with wooden cleats, would be considered unsafe by today's standards. During the football season, the cleats would wear down until the nails that held them in place protruded. More injuries were caused by cleats than by tackles. Throughout my entire football career, I don't remember getting a new pair of football shoes.

Football Days as a Quarterback

My coach placed me in the quarterback's position, and I was known as a triple-threat quarterback. A triple-threat quarterback is one who has the ability to pass, run, or punt the football, depending on the play. Our football team's style of play was patterned after the 1930s Notre Dame football team, so we didn't huddle to get a play. To start the play, I would line up behind either the right or left guard with three backs behind me and bark out numbers, such as 32, 24, 35, hut one, hut two, hut three, until the ball was snapped. Each number was significant; the first digit of the first number would be the snap signal. At times, we would change the snap signal to the second number to confuse opponents who thought they had scouted us well. The other numbers made up the play.

After football practice, we were allowed to quench our thirst, and boy, were we thirsty. No water was available on the practice field, so my teammates and I would climb a nearby hill to drink the clear, cool water running from a mountain spring called Dry Bones Spring. It was named Dry Bones because it ran through an old cemetery. Recalling those moments, I wonder if that spring water contained potent vitamins or even age-retardants, as almost every guy on my team who drank from Dry Bones Spring lived to be in his late eighties or nineties.

Even though the games of basketball and football have evolved to a much higher level in such a short time frame, some aspects of the games have remained the same. The spirit of the games, the enthusiasm of spectators, and the life lessons gleaned from competition are the same today as they were in the 1930s.

Mullens Walker Esso Independent Basketball Team
1st Row L-R Shorty Prichard, Louie Rezzonico, Jay Warden,
Andy Pendalton, Al Morgan, Jack Finney
2nd Row L-R Bill Rezzonico, F.S. Calfee, Lewis D'Antoni,
not identified

Early Transportation

Chapter Eight:

College and Semipro Baseball Years

My father was my primary role model. He did not tell me what to do or how to do things; he showed me. His work ethic, his approach to difficult challenges, and the way he conducted himself throughout his life were the standards I subconsciously set for myself as I matured into a young man.

Another person who influenced my life was Coach Woodell, my high school basketball coach, who later became my college basketball coach during my junior and senior years. A great teacher and a good coach, Coach Woodell didn't really talk or spend time with me, but he was someone I admired as I watched the way he lived his life. By observing him, I learned the same as I learned from my father, by actions, not by words. This influence was so monumental that I decided to follow in his footsteps. He was a biology teacher and a coach, so I became a biology teacher and a coach.

After high school, I received an offer of a four-year basketball and football scholarship from Coach Pedie Jackson at Emery and Henry College and a four-year basketball and football scholarship from Concord College. I accepted Concord's offer because it was closer to home and many students from Mullens went to that college.

High School Graduation

Di decided to go further away from home for college. He received a four-year football scholarship from Coach Cam Henderson at Marshall College in Huntington, West Virginia. During his playing years at Marshall, he was the starting quarterback of the Marshall football team and was later inducted into Marshall's Athletic Hall of Fame.

While at Concord, I lettered all four years in football, basketball, and tennis, leaving little free time for other activities. (Concord did not offer organized baseball at that time or I would have really been stretched for time.) My scholarship included room and board, but part of the agreement was that I had to work. Being a freshman, I had the dirtiest job: washing pots and pans. My sophomore year, I graduated to cleaning the silverware. My third year, I gave up the kitchen duty and moved to the more appealing job of lining off the tennis courts. Finally, in my senior year, I was assigned to the most prestigious job of all: winding the electric clock in the gym. At that point, I knew I had reached the big time.

Number 32 on College Football Team

Outside of sports, my social activities included fraternity life. I was a member of the Phi Delta Pi, the fraternity
with all the "jocks." To become a fraternity brother, I was
required to participate in hell week, which really tested my
"coraggio"(mettle).

At the start of hell week, I was required to walk to Bennett's
mountain, five miles from the school, and build a fire so large
that the flames could be seen by the fraternity brothers who
were at the college. To build a large fire, we had to find and
carry wood from several miles away because of all the fires
that had been built during the previous hell weeks.

Another day, we were dropped at a farm three miles from
the school. We were given a gunny sack and were required
to carry it back to the college after we had filled it with at
least fifty pounds of manure. As we loaded it into the sack, it
was watered down by some of the fraternity members. The
sack was weighed at the destination, and if it was under the
required weight, we were punished and had to roll a peanut
with our nose up the college sidewalk for about twenty-five
yards. After that ordeal, we were taken by car to Princeton,
about twenty miles away, and let out. Our orders were to find
a way back to the college and on the way to count the number
of telephone poles so we could report the number when we
returned.

The grand finale of hell week was even worse. We were
allowed to wear our shorts but no shoes or shirts. At various
stations located around the room were electric paddles they
used to send electric currents through our bodies. The worst
part of hell week was the last event. Pledges were paired
and required to stand together at a window. Each of us were
handed a pair of scissors and a brick with a long string tied
around it. With each partner having a turn, we were required
to attach the loose end of the string tied to the brick to our
manhood. Standing side by side with our partner, we were
instructed to drop the brick out of the three-story window.
Your partner's role was to cut the string after you dropped

the brick. Believe me, this gave a whole new meaning to trust and to having your teammate's "back." My worst fear was that I would hear the words, "I am so sorry!"

Fraternity life was fun and, thankfully, physically uneventful. And it introduced me to dancing, an activity not associated with sports that I enjoyed in college. When I started college, I did not know how to dance, but I learned quickly and really enjoyed the dances that were held. I don't think I ever missed one. My favorite dance routine was called the Concord Hop, and it required fancy foot work to maneuver your partner across the floor.

For the dances held around Mullens, Betty Jo was my partner of choice. But I do have to admit that Carl Clifford, who was a good friend and a good dancer too, made an excellent, if not a little strange, dance partner. He and I always managed to dance at least once during a neighborhood party and were acclaimed as the best couple on the floor. Outside of sports, dancing became my favorite pastime. While I cannot participate in a game of basketball now, I can still cut a mean rug on the dance floor. It just requires the help of my "trainer," Jack Daniels.

Another nonsports dimension added to my life in college was dating. Unlike most young men who start dating in their teenage years, I did not date in high school. I was too busy playing sports, which took all of my interest and time. While in college, I began to date. It took time getting use to the process, but I learned quickly and really enjoyed dating. I went steady with two girls, at different times of course, while at Concord. Like me, none of my sons were very active in the high school dating scene. Fortunately, in high school, my sons' interest in sports was stronger than their admiration for the opposite sex. However, again like me, they wasted no time in catching up once they started college.

I am a firm believer that young high school ballplayers should devote their time and energies to their game. For boys who date in high school, it confuses their young psyches, and as a coach, it is hard to deal with ballplayers who have the "sweet ass" or "moon eyes."

In May 1937, I graduated from college and was hired by the Wyoming County Board of Education as a biology teacher and basketball coach at Pineville High School to replace Pete Elmo Morgan, who later became my brother-in-law.

My First High School Basketball Team as a Coach Pineville did not have a football team, so in 1938, I organized and coached a six-man football team.
1st Row L-R Carl Brazzie, Harry Jackson, Walter Greene, Jr. Rose, Coy Rose
2nd Row L-R Al Morgan Dolan Manning, Seth Phillips, Bryon Rose
3rd Row L-R Asst. Coach Woodrow Harper, Lowell Roberts, Benton Stewart, Woodrow Rutherford, Coach Lewis D'Antoni

During the winter months, in addition to my coaching duties, I played on an independent basketball team. Its members—Paul Goode, Clarence Shufflebarger, Woody Cook, Orville Goins, Harold Dooley, Curtis Crotty, and myself—were all from Mullens and had played basketball in college. We were called the Dr. Peppers and were sponsored by the Dr. Pepper Bottling Company. As a sponsor, they purchased our wool jerseys. Throughout the Appalachian region, towns would organize games between the various independent teams in an effort to raise money for schools. To get to the games, we borrowed cars from the Long Wells dealership in Mullens. On a trip to Honeaker, Virginia, we had to wad newspapers around the door and windows to keep warm. When we arrived at the gym, Shuff, our driver (who always provided us with thrilling rides), backed our car up against a tree. I asked Shuff why he was parking the car there, and he stated the brakes in the car were not working very well.

The Dr. Pepper Team (front row L-R, Paul Goode, Curt Crotty, Harold Dooley, back row L-R, Lewis D'Antoni, Clarence Shufflebarger, Woody Cook

Along with the independent basketball games in the region, there were a large number of independent tournaments scheduled. The most popular were the Gold Medal Tournaments. At these tournaments, gold medals were given to the highest scorer, best sport, winning team, most rebounds, and so on. Our team won the majority of tournaments we entered, and each of us had a nice collection of gold medals. My stint in independent basketball teams and tournaments lasted five years.

During the spring months after football and basketball season, I played semipro baseball. The county school system granted me a leave of absence to play with the Class D Bluefield Blue Grays of the Mountain State League. I was voted the most popular player in the league and was given a nice wristwatch. Years later, to my surprise, I discovered that during my third year on the Blue Grays team, my .369 batting average was higher than an opponent who played at the same time on the Williamson team. His name was Stan Musial.

Team travel, unpredictable at best, was either by bus or by individual cars. In the 1930s, the roads in West Virginia were hazardous. In fact, I was lucky to have survived the trips and make it to my third year of baseball. For travel to our away games, the Class D league furnished a team bus for us. Returning from a game in Williamson, West Virginia, we had to travel in the bus over several mountains to reach Bluefield. The last mountain was a doozy. We were approximately one-third of the way down the mountain when the brakes on the bus became hot and stopped working. The bus started moving very fast down the mountain, its speed increasing second by second, the driver fighting the steering wheel as he maneuvered the bus through the curves. He took the curves to the outside and then back to the inside as we twisted our way down the mountain in a runaway bus. Without working brakes, the bus was careening, its tires screeching, and all of us were rolling on the floor, holding on to the foot of the seats, each other, or anything else we could grab to help stabilize our bodies. We were yelling, screaming, and praying. Fortunately, we did not meet another vehicle, like a giant coal truck that used the route often coming up the mountain. Finally, we made it to the bottom safely, and the bus slowly drifted to a stop. Pandemonium ceased. Immediately, an eerie quietness overcame the bus. The realization of

My Semi-pro Baseball Years with the Blue Grays

My Semi-pro Baseball Years with the Blue Grays

what could have happened sunk in and we were grateful to be on level ground. In retrospect, I don't think I ever came so close to ending my life—and that includes my time in World War II.

In my last year with the Bluefield Blue Grays, the ballpark was equipped with regular lights. It was the first one in the area to have lights. Prior to that, companies would bring in Delco lights. These lights were run by a generator, which proved to be a little tricky. If it was operating correctly, the generator produced bright lights adequate for the game, but at times, it would sputter or slow down, causing the lights to blink and dim. Playing centerfield under the Delco lights proved to be a somewhat challenging and dangerous situation. But it did keep me alert.

Bluefield had a makeshift ballpark. In left field, the park had a small hill about 230 feet from home plate. There was a path around the center of the hill where the left outfielder stood. To hit a homerun to left field, the batter needed to hit a ball that would not only clear the hill but also the outfielder standing on the hill. In center field, where I played, the homerun area was a grove of trees and bushes located directly behind center field, about 320 feet from home plate. A homerun to right field was 330 feet to the fence.

One night, I was taking outfield practice before a game, and my manager walked up to me with a baseball in his hand and told me to find an area in the grove of trees where I could hide the ball. He further said that if I just happened to find *a* ball after a batter on the opposing team hit one into the grove of trees, well, who was to say it was not the ball that had just been hit? Reluctantly, but doing as I was told, I found a nice spot in the trees for the ball. It was the third inning of the game and the score was tied. A ball was hit hard, rising over my outstretched hand. Into the grove of trees and bushes it flew. On cue, I ran back into the bushes, quickly retrieved *a* ball, and to the total astonishment of the runner and the opponent's dugout, threw him out as he rounded third heading for home. What a great throw!

I laugh now recalling the incident, but I must say I felt rather guilty for a long while.

Eventually, I was sold to the Portsmouth Class B baseball team for $500, and in 1941, was given a tryout with the Albany Class A team managed by Rabbit Marivelle. But a pro career was not to be in my future, as I was told by the Albany management that I was too old to play. Since I was twenty-seven years old, Albany decided not to take a chance on me. A little disappointed, I returned to Bluefield and played another year.

In the spring season of my last professional baseball season, I was preparing to leave school and head to Bluefield when I became ill with the flu. Still living with Dad, who was working long hours, I was basically alone in the house and too sick to take care of myself. Paul Goode, the county sheriff and a resident of Mullens, was a good friend of mine. We played basketball together while I was in college, and he invited me to stay with him and his wife Kathleen until I recovered from the flu. Accepting his invitation, I temporarily moved into his home. Also living with Kat and Paul at the time was Betty Jo Bailey, Kat's younger sister.

Arriving at their home, Kat showed me to my bedroom, and all I wanted to do was to go to bed. I felt awful. As I laid my head on the pillow and closed my eyes, Betty Jo entered the room. Kat had sent her in to check on me to see if I needed anything. I slowly opened my eyes and focused on Betty Jo, who was standing at the foot of my bed. Even through my flu-laden eyes, I could see that she was the most beautiful girl I had ever encountered. My heart started to race wildly, and it was not because of the flu.

For the next two weeks, Betty Jo was my nurse. The flu lasted much longer than was normal because I had no desire to give up her attentive behavior. But the time came when I could fake it no longer, as I had to return to my baseball team. Reluctantly, I left. I said my thank-yous and good-byes to everyone. Even though I was leaving her now, I promised myself that my nurse would become a permanent fixture in my life.

Pictures of Betty Jo

Chapter Nine:

Marriage and the War Years

Icontinued to coach basketball at Pineville High School and to play semipro baseball, but I managed to adjust my schedule to include time for dating. And the only person I was interested in was Betty Jo. We dated for about a year before we decided to get married. At that time, marrying an Italian was not a common occurrence. Kate, her mother, really liked me and was agreeable to the marriage. However, Cal, her father, wasn't too sure. After Betty Jo agreed to marry me, her father jokingly remarked, "Well, I hope that when you have kids, the half that's American is the half that talks."

Our elopement to Bristol, Virginia, was not a secret. Instead, we were accompanied by two carloads of people, including Kate Bailey, Betty Jo's mother; Kat Goode and Garnett Lee Morgan, her two sisters; Paul Goode, Kat's husband; and Helen and Clarence (Shuff) Shufflebarger, our close friends. We were almost to our destination when Shuff, who was riding in the backseat, hollered, "Stop the car." Fearing trouble, I immediately slammed on the brakes. Throwing the door open, he jumped out of the car, hopped over a fence on the side of the road and ran into a large field full of wild flowers. The group in the cars watched in bewilderment as Shuff furiously began picking wild flowers. With arms so full that flowers were spilling out of his arms, he climbed back over the fence. Getting in the car, wild flowers dropping everywhere, he stated, "Hell, Lewis, you can't have a wedding without flowers. We can go now." We were official; our wedding had lots of flowers, wild and beautiful.

The First Presbyterian Church, in Bristol was the site of our intimate wedding, with Reverend Brown presiding. After the ceremony, we were famished, so on our way back to Mullens, the small wedding party stopped in Bluefield, West Virginia to enjoy a spaghetti dinner at Jimmy's Italian restaurant. This was the first of spaghetti dinners too numerous to count. It set a tradition in our home for family and friends during our married life. Today, I still have spaghetti sauce simmering on my stove in Mullens.

Betty Jo and I had no home of our own in Mullens, so Curt and Pauline Crotty, our friends, offered us theirs for our wedding night. When we were getting ready for bed that night, we discovered not only had they short-sheeted the bed but had placed salt and coat hangers between the sheets. An hour after cleaning up the mess, we finally climbed into bed. No sooner were we settled when the phone began to ring. I answered. It was Curt. "Hey, Lewis. How are you doing?" I could hear the rest of our wedding party giggling in the background.

Laughingly, I answered "Fine!" and hung up. The telephone game went on every half hour for most of the night. Sadly, I must admit that we were so naïve and dumb that we continued to answer the phone, never once thinking to take it off the hook. Finally, in the wee hours of the morning, they left us alone. The next day, I played in a semipro baseball game out-of-town and hit a home run—again!

By living in a small town in West Virginia, most people were insulated from the events taking place across the nation. Everyone in the small town read about the stock market crash, and the bank failures affected us to a certain degree. However, our little community survived them. Although we listened to the fireside chats of President Franklin Delano Roosevelt, we continued our daily lives as we had for the past years. Dad continued to work his successful business, and the Mullens economy continued to hum via the mines and railroads. Unlike so many other places in the United States, we were basically isolated from the horrible miseries the rest of the country was experiencing.

In 1941, one event penetrated our protected mountain barrier, and it was one that could not isolate us from the rest of the nation. In fact, it shook the small town of Mullens to its roots. It was World War II. Disrupting the daily routine of Mullens, it uprooted its male population, including me and brother Di, and transported us to foreign countries to defend our nation. Even my sister Olga joined the WAVES, Women Accepted for Volunteer Emergency Services. Many buddies, my siblings, and I left our small town and took care of national business. Gratefully, most of us returned to Mullens four years later. The war that created the Greatest Generation sent us home changed, but in many ways we stayed the same.

One morning during the war years, Rosie remarked to my dad, "How can you sleep at night knowing your two sons and daughter are fighting in the war?"

Dad proudly replied, "Our family ina battle to help our country. Ima proud of my kids. So, I sleep easy."

As World War II unfolded, Di enlisted in the Army Air Corp. He was a pilot during the war, flying ninety-two missions and earning the Distinguished Flying Cross Medal. Di flew a P-40 fighter aircraft and was a squadron leader. On July 4, 1943, returning from a mission, Di's squadron was attacked by German fighter planes. Even though his squadron was heavily outnumbered, they were successful in repelling the Germans. During the air battle, Di observed that his wingman had been separated from the squadron and was under enemy fire from more than one German plane. Although Di's plane had been damaged in the skirmish, he went to the aid of his comrade. In the ensuing battle, Di shot down an enemy plane, freeing his wingman from the situation and saving his life.

The war was the first time I had been separated from my family. I did not have the same interest in flying as Di, so I joined the navy. I was assigned to the Seabees; promoted to the rank of ensign, and sent to Tucson, Arizona, for training. After I graduated from naval training in Arizona, I was transferred to New York for gunnery school. The last stage of my training took place in Norfolk, Virginia, close to home and my family.

Officers Training Class of '42

I really missed Betty Jo during this period, so we devised a plan to meet each other. The war efforts restricted travel, and gasoline was rationed. But somehow Betty Jo secured five five-gallon cans of gasoline, which she carried in the trunk of the car, and drove to Norfolk. Pregnant with our first child and fearless, she drove twelve hours to see me. I managed to get a two-hour pass. When she stepped out of that car, boy, did she look good to me!

In October, while I was still in training at the naval base in Norfolk, I got a call from Paul Goode telling me that Betty Jo was ready to give birth to our first child. Excited, I immediately went to my commander to ask for leave. Upon requesting a week's furlough, he responded, "Mr. D'Antoni, you were necessary for the laying of the keel, but, sir, you are not needed for the launching." My leave was denied. In a few days, the launch was successful, our daughter Kathy was born, and I was granted leave.

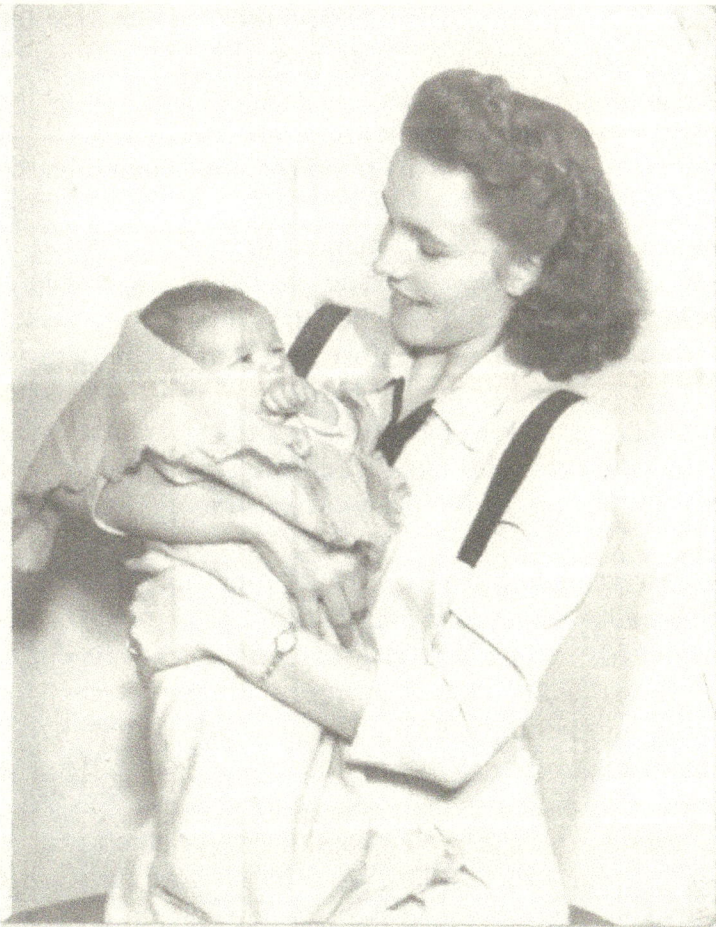

Betty Jo and Our First Born, Kathy

I returned to Norfolk, and after my training was complete, my next post was aboard a LST 585 in Pensacola, Florida. After a shakedown cruise, our LST was loaded with ammunition and supplies. Our crew of several hundred took off from Biloxi, Mississippi, through the Panama Canal and headed for the war in the Pacific. Only fourteen of the hundred-man crew had been to sea, and the captain, a former school teacher, had very little experience, facts that didn't encourage confidence.

Shortly into the cruise off the coast of Florida, we hit the tail end of a hurricane. The ship had a flat bottom, which caused an extremely rough ride, and most of the crew, including me, became seasick. My duty post was the conning tower, and I still have vivid memories of standing duty with a bucket tightly gripped in my hand. I don't think I ate for two days, and that memory is as fresh in my mind today as when it happened seventy years ago.

After eighteen hours, we made it to the Panama Canal and then headed for the New Hebrides Islands. As I stood high over the water at my post and watched the glimmering lights disappear from view, a sick feeling rose slowly in the pit of my stomach. Faced with the cruelty of battles and war, I wondered if I would make it back to Betty Jo and my family. Remembering the adversity my father had faced time after time, I found the resolve within me to fulfill my sworn duty and to ultimately survive.

After serving in the navy for forty-four months, with fifteen months in the Pacific, on September 1945 I received orders to return home. The war was over! People were euphoric. Celebrations broke out everywhere. Seaman were dancing, cheering, and jumping off the boat into the waters. Everyone was more than ready to return home. While docked in Manila, Philippines, I was given orders to board the *USS Thomas Paine* for my return trip. Needless to say, I couldn't wait to get home. But, wait I did, as the ship took fifty-five days to return to the States. I experienced the true meaning of a "slow boat to China."

Finally, I was discharged from the navy on January 2, 1946, almost four years after I enlisted. I boarded a train from Pensacola, Florida, to Welch, West Virginia, where Betty Jo, Kathy (my four-year-old daughter whom I had only seen once), and Paul Goode (my brother-in-law) were patiently waiting. What a wonderful day. At ninety-five, I can still recall the incredible excitement of being home for good and resuming life with my family.

Once home, I enrolled at Marshall University where I earned a master's in education administration. After completing my degree, I was hired by the Wyoming County School System as a football, basketball, and baseball coach and a health teacher at Mullens High School. We rented a small house in Mullens. Kathy was almost five, and Betty Jo was eight months pregnant with our second child.

On July 9, 1947, Lewis Joseph D'Antoni, II, my first son, was born. To avoid the confusion caused by having the same name as mine, folks began referring to him as Little Dan. Eventually, the nickname Little Dan evolved into Danny.

The addition to our family created cramped living quarters in our small home, and Betty Jo and I began looking for a new place to live. After visiting his firstborn grandson, Dad called us together. As a gift, he handed Betty Jo and me the deed to the home he had built for his family nineteen years earlier. Thrilled beyond words, we moved into the brick home on Moran Avenue that over the years has created so many wonderful memories. Two of those wonderful times were May 8, 1951, the birth of Michael Andrew, my second son, and ten years later, October 31, 1961, to the surprise of Betty Jo, who thought I was too old to have children, Mark Bailey, our third son was born.

The D'Antoni Men (L to R Danny, Lewis, Mark, and Mike)

The Family (First Row L-R Anna (my sister) Betty Jo, Mike, Second Row L-R Kathy, Lewis, Danny, and Mark

Chapter Ten:

Betty Jo

My coaching years were fun, exciting, and successful in large part because of the girl I married. A bit of my advice for young folks: coaches need to marry a certain type of lady, one who understands the multifaceted environment of a coach's life. Basketball presents the coach with a full and eventful ride. During the season, coaches live through major highs and lows. Emotional swings dominate, and by season's end, the coach is left physically and emotionally drained. The off-season and downtime away from the game must be low-key, with few demands. It is a time to rest so the body can recharge.

Betty Jo made a great coach's wife. She did not allow me to waller (a good ol' West Virginia expression) in my misery if we lost or to bask in my victory if we won. She would allow for about ten minutes of rehashing the game and then it was time for a diversion, which would be another form of competition. She knew the only way to get my mind off one game was to start a new one. Competition in coaches is like oxygen in blood. It is so interrelated within your being that you have to require it to feel alive. Betty Jo understood that, and I can still hear her in my mind saying, "Okay, that's enough about

the game, let's see what you can really do. Let's play bridge!"
And the card table would go up, the cards would appear, and
another competition was started

Not only was Betty Jo a competitor and loved sports as
much as I did, she had great athletic skills. I could never boast
that our kids got their athletic ability just from me. In fact,
she was so athletic that in the late '30s during her freshman
year in high school, she was a starter on the Baileysville High
School boys' basketball team. Not enough boys tried out to fill
the team roster that year, so the basketball coach asked Betty
Jo to play. She was a very good player and usually scored a lot
of points; however, the boys claimed that she had an advantage
because no one dared to guard her close. In the 1930s, social
mores were a lot different than today, and she played this to
her advantage. She started on the team for one year and then
transferred from Baileysville High School to Mullens High
School, giving up her organized basketball playing days.

Basketball was only one of her talents. Betty Jo was a good
bowler, played first base on a softball team, was elected as head
cheerleader for the high school teams, and was an outstanding
tennis player. When she was ten years old and visiting Texas,
she won a singles match against the Texas State Junior Tennis
Champion.

A stickler for rules, she played to win both in sports and in
life. As a fan, she lived every moment of the action on the floor.
In the beginning of my coaching career, Betty Jo never missed
a game and was always in the stands, but that changed one
fateful night. Mullens was playing a fierce basketball rival, and
the gym was packed with spectators. The two referees for the
game were close friends of our family, and in fact, Paul Vennari,
one of the refs, had eaten dinner with us the night before. A
great game unfolded that night as two outstanding teams were
pitted against each other. The fans were not disappointed by
the exciting game. With twenty seconds to go in the game, the
score was tied, and we had the ball after a timeout. Our point
guard dribbled across the center line and an opposing player

Betty Jo, A Fierce Competitior at age 10 In her teenage years, she and her sister Helen won the West Virginia Women's Tennis Doubles title.

reached in, trying to swat the ball away. It came loose and both players dove after the ball. With one second on the clock, Paul blew his whistle, and before everyone's unbelieving eyes, called a foul on our player. The opponent went to the foul line and immediately sunk two free throws, ending the ball game.

The crowd reacted. Our fans were standing at their seats, dazed and trying to process what had taken place, while the opponents were wildly cheering and screaming victoriously. Betty Jo, who had been standing in disbelief with the crowd, began to make her way through the rush of people leaving the gym. As she inched her way through the crowd to the gym door, she came face-to-face with Paul Vennari. He made the mistake of asking Betty Jo how she liked the game. Without warning, Betty Jo smacked Paul with her open hand. The sound was heard by the exiting crowd and everyone stopped to stare. Betty Jo suddenly realized what she had done and hurried out the door and rushed home. Ashamed and upset at herself and her aggressive actions, she stopped going to my games. It was the last high school ball game Betty Jo ever attended. She missed all three of her sons' high school and college games until twenty years later when she agreed to go to some of Mike's games at Marshall. Paul Vennari remained a good friend. He was a good ref, but that night, a reach-in foul should have been called against the opponent. Our player should have been the one shooting the fouls for the win. Way to go, Betty Jo.

The incident with Paul Vennari for Betty Jo was an ah-ha moment in her life. She realized what it meant to be so emotionally involved in the moment that you lose your perspective on the total experience. From that time on, she made it a priority to divorce herself from the extreme emotions of the game and to keep her husband and children focused on the big picture and not to get lost in the moment, whether it was winning or losing.

Competition was the staple in our household. There was always some type of competitive game going on. Basketball, board games, cards—all were involved. Rules were followed, and no one cheated, as that was the death knell in our house. Not even in fun was cheating permitted.

Betty Jo and I did not let our children win. If you won a game in our house, you earned it. The winner of all the games were proudly updated and posted on the refrigerator for all to see. The list remained day in and day out, waiting to either be confirmed or to reveal a new champion. Our neighbors always knew when a new winner was posted because of all the yelling, laughing, and loud talking escaping from our kitchen. Winning gave you bragging rights until the next game, which was never too far off. All family members were on a level playing field.

The greatest lessons we taught our children were (1) Always play by the rules. Winning by cheating is a hollow victory. It deprives you of dignity and self-respect, and it will eventually come back to haunt you. And (2) victories or losses do not define you; they are only moments in time to either be enjoyed and celebrated or to allow the opportunity to regroup and devise a new strategy.

What I remember most about our family life together was the love and laughter that never took a break. Love was shown often, openly, and respectfully. In our home, love ran deep and was fun as long as everyone understood he or she was part of a whole and not the whole part. This concept was reinforced often, both with my children and with my ball clubs. Betty Jo's philosophy on raising children was reflected in her comments, "I am not raising my children to like me; I am raising my children so others will like them." We taught our children respect for others, how to enjoy their lives, how to have fun with each other, and what it meant to have a sense of humor, especially the ability to laugh at oneself.

The ability to laugh at oneself was unexpectedly taught to a wedding guest in our home, much to Betty Jo's dismay. It was the morning of our daughter Kathy's wedding day. The wedding party had arrived the night before. Kathy was worried about the best man because his nose was extremely large and he was very sensitive about its size. Since he was a guest in her home, which housed the world's biggest kidders, Kathy was concerned that someone would slip and make a teasing comment. She just knew her brothers would make jokes or tease him about his nose, so she had spent the week constantly warning everyone not to say anything. The day before everyone arrived, Betty Jo became impatient with all of Kathy's warnings and she remarked, "How can you think we would hurt anyone's feelings? Not in my house. Not as long as I am the mother here. So just hush up about it and let's have a good time." Kathy agreed but was still nervous.

It was now the morning of the wedding, and all had arrived. Everyone, as usual, had gathered in the kitchen, and hot steaming coffee, scrambled eggs, biscuits with jellies, and mimosas in champagne flutes were being served. The mood was festive, with folks laughing and talking, and Betty Jo was being the perfect hostess, watching over everyone and taking care of their needs. With a full coffee pot in her hand, she was going from guest to guest refilling coffee cups. Approaching the best man, Betty Jo leaned over to pour his coffee. Looking him dead in the eyes, she sweetly asked, "Honey, do you take cream and sugar with your nose?" All conversations stopped. Silence engulfed the kitchen. No one moved. Frozen where she stood with coffee pot in hand, Betty Jo's face was covered in total shock. After what seemed like an eternity, the best man began to laugh, softly at first and then into a full-belly laugh. The entire kitchen erupted into laughter as Betty Jo stood there in total dismay. Later, Betty Jo claimed if Kathy had not warned everyone so many times about his nose, the situation would never have happened. I assured Betty Jo she should not worry; we all knew it was Kathy's fault.

Chapter Eleven:

Mike, Danny, and the Other Children

Christmas Day, 1954. Snow was falling, covering the mountains. A fire was crackling in the living room fireplace, and presents were stacked under the ceiling-high tree. Santa Claus has arrived, and a perfect Christmas morning was in the making. Through the quiet, a female child's voice was heard, "Daddy, what time is it?"

Sleepily, I answered, "It's ten minutes past the last time you asked me." It was Christmas morning at the D'Antoni's, and Kathy, acting as the spokesperson for the young trio of children, was asking for the third time if they could go downstairs to see if Santa had visited the house.

Waiting a few seconds, I remarked playfully, "Okay, I give up. You can get up now!" Shrieks of joy came from Kathy's bedroom where she, Danny, and Mike had congregated. It was the traditional Christmas morning ritual. Sometime in the wee hours of day, usually around 4:00 AM on Christmas morning, the two boys would make their way to Kathy's bedroom, crawl into bed with her, and wait together for permission to get up and go downstairs to see what presents Santa had brought.

Unlike the wide-awake children who impatiently waited outside our door, Betty Jo and I, still half asleep, walked wearily from our bedroom. It was way too early to begin the day. We delivered Santa about three hours earlier and knew the day would be hectic, filled with visiting relatives and friends. Stopping outside our bedroom door, I smiled at seeing our three children sitting side by side on the first step of the long staircase, quietly talking in excited tones about all the wonderful treasures and possibilities that lay ahead for them. Kathy, the oldest and only daughter, was sitting on one end. The self-appointed protector of the younger boys, Kathy still views this as her role in life. Seated at the other end of the trio was Danny, our oldest son, spunky, energetic, a true daredevil. He was busy talking with Mike, who was carefully sandwiched protectively between his two older siblings. He was an easygoing child, intelligent, compassionate, and full of fun. He was listening to every word Danny was telling him. As they heard Betty Jo and I approach, the Christmas ritual began. Kathy, Danny, and Mike, holding hands, descended the steps together, one at a time, all on the same step, with Betty Jo and me following close behind. They remained together, holding hands and moving in tandem with each other into the room where the beautiful tree topped with the Christmas angel, which was required to touch the ceiling, held all the Christmas treasures.

My children, including Mark, who was born later but entered the tight circle without skipping a beat, have all traveled through life this way, holding hands, seeking the endless treasures and possibilities, always as excited for each other as they are for themselves. Not only are they siblings, but they are each other's best friends. Endowed with similar traits, they are equally competitive, gregarious, fun-loving, humorous, quick-witted, risk-taking, and—most importantly—compassionate. All love competitive games, either as a participant or as a spectator. As the years pass, their bond continues to strengthen, even though distance has separated them. They talk to each other at least twice a week, keeping attuned to the others lives.

Being a father, I was always conscious of the public's view of my children's successes. Knowing that I was fortunate to be their principal and coach, I did not want other students to think that I favored them in any activities that I supervised. So, when they earned a school honor or acquired a position on the basketball team, they had to work harder than the others. I wanted no one to argue that my children succeeded because of who they were.

I was the principal of the school that my children attended, and their teachers were aware of my feelings. However, one teacher found a way to circumvent my views. An essay contest was held by the local Rotary Club with an award of $100 given to the best writer. As principal, my role was to select the winning essay from a group of five finalists. Unbeknown to me, Mike's essay was among the finalists. Mrs. Kaman, the teacher in charge of the contest, knew that regardless of how good Mike's entry was, I would never select it for first place because of how some may see it as favoritism. To make certain that the contest was fair for Mike, Mrs. Kaman removed all the names from the papers before she brought them in for me to judge. After reading all the essays, I told Mrs. Kaman that one paper stood out from all the rest and that student should win the award, and I handed her the winning paper. Mrs. Kaman looked at the winning essay and promptly responded, "Good choice. And by the way, you selected your son's paper."

I am extremely proud that I can honestly say that each one of my children, on their own merit, has been successful in their chosen endeavors. And because of their individual successes, they have managed to keep each other grounded by remembering their roots. Mike and Danny, to a lesser degree, are the ones who have experienced the most national acclaim, but their siblings are quick to point out they too have succeeded— and not by dribbling a ball. There is an ongoing joke between Kathy and Mark concerning all the articles written about Mike and Danny. In most of the articles, the author refers to Mike and Danny's accomplishments, awards, and honors, and usually mentions me and my basketball achievements. At the end of the articles, there is usually a statement that says "and the other children are …" So, for the past three or four years, Kathy and Mark affectionately refer to themselves as "the other children."

Affection in our household is displayed through acts of teasing. Betty Jo taught our children at an early age to be able to laugh at themselves, to be confident in their own worth, and to be able to dish it back to the one creating the joke. If you were the butt of jokes in our home, you were well liked. If you were not, basic manners would be followed. It is difficult to explain the camaraderie that comes from the ability to joke with others without taking it as a personal affront. Plus, I have observed that the bantering between my children has kept their egos at the right level.

The bantering continues in their adult lives. Recently, Kathy called Danny to tell him about the tennis tournament she had entered. Kathy likes to remind her brothers that even though she is the oldest, at least her body and reflexes have not aged as fast as some other people she knows. Excited about the tennis match, Kathy reported, "Hey, Danny, I made it to the women's doubles finals in the tennis tournament. It was a great game. We split sets against the opponents and the game was decided by a super tiebreaker. Unfortunately, we lost by two points in the tiebreaker, but I was happy. I played well, and we got these beautiful runners-up trophies. Isn't that great?"

Danny quickly responded, "Hey, gal, that's super! I don't think we have one of those trophies in our family!"

I also remember the time Mike left Italy to join the Denver Nuggets as the person in charge of player personnel. His salary was going to be less than he was used to making in Italy as a professional basketball player and coach, and he was putting together a household budget when he decided to share his woes with Danny. At the time, Danny was a high school coach at Socastee High School in the Myrtle Beach area, raising three boys, and scraping financially to make ends meet. The phone conversation went like this.

"Hey, Mike, what's up?"

"Not much. I tell you, it is hard to live on a budget. I'm trying to decide if I should get first-class seats to Seattle or just travel coach."

Danny hung up the phone.

Mike called again. "Danny, something happened to the phone line, I was talking about my salary cut and budgets—"

Danny hung up the phone again.

Mike called back for the third time. "Danny, what's going on? Why are you hanging up on me?"

"Well," Danny quipped, "you're calling me and trying to decide whether or not you can fly first class. I'm sitting here trying to decide if I can have pepperoni on my pizza! Mike, you really need to call someone else!"

The boys are not the only athletes in the family. Kathy was a great athlete who, unfortunately, was born before Proposition 9. The opportunities for her at a young age were not available, so her athletic prowess was not developed to its full potential. But she still competes toe-to-toe with her brothers, winning her fair share.

Kathy was fresh out of college and working as a teacher at Oceana High School. The principal asked her to coach the girls' basketball team. I guess, because of her family, he thought it would be a good fit. Even though Kathy had never coached before, she was confident she could handle the job. She asked me for advice about basketball plays, practice drills, how to run her offense and defense, and all of the elements of being a good coach. I worked with her as she developed her philosophy and game plan, and every day after practice she would question me on various situations.

Finally, the day arrived for her coaching debut. The first game of the season was on their home court. And, to show family support, Mike, Danny, and I attended the game.

The gymnasium was packed with spectators. It was the opening game of the season and Oceana, Kathy's team, was playing their archrival, Pineville High School. The D'Antoni well-wishers made their way to the top row of the bleachers in order to have a good view of the action. Kathy was giving last minute instructions to her team when the referee blew the whistle indicating it was time to start the game. The team huddle broke and starters for both teams came to midcourt for the tip-off.

The referee proceeded with the regulation jump ball. The opponents retrieved the opening tip-off and quickly dribbled to their basket and scored. Unfortunately, this same pattern continued for the next two to three minutes of the game. Kathy's team would inbound the ball after the opponent's scored, quickly move to their basket, shoot, and miss. The opponents would rebound the ball, move the ball toward their end of the floor, and shoot, making the basket. We sat there watching as the scoring continued to mount for Pineville: 2-0, 4-0, 6-0, 10-0, 12-0. Pineville was having their way with the Oceana team as Kathy sat quietly on the bench.

As the score continued to increase for Pineville, a note written on a small piece of paper began making its way from the top of the bleachers, down through the crowd, to the Oceana bench. A spectator sitting directly behind Kathy tapped her on the shoulder and handed her the traveling note. Kathy slowly opened the note to read what her brothers had written: "Call time-out, stupid!" Looking up at them from the bench with a look of befuddlement on her face, Kathy shrugged her shoulders. It dawned on me she didn't know how to call a time-out. After all the instructions I had given her on how to win the game, I had neglected to tell her how a coach calls time-out. Laughing at the thought, I sighed in relief when the opposing coach, who could not resist coaching a little, called a time-out. Kathy observed and learned. She lost her opening debut as a coach, but she went on that year to win the county high school girls championship.

As I mentioned, after they became adults and were on their own, my children continued to find ways to be together.

Danny moved out of West Virginia to accept a coaching position at Socastee High School in the Myrtle Beach area. It wasn't long before he convinced Kathy to move to Myrtle Beach too, and Mike, who was playing professional basketball in Italy, spent the off-season with them in South Carolina. Finally, Mark "decided" to go to college at Coastal Carolina College, which is located just outside of Myrtle Beach. Actually, Mark received a four-year basketball scholarship to attend Coastal, so his "decision" may have been slightly influenced by his parents.

During one summer, my kids came up with an intriguing idea. Evidently, Mike's earnings from his rooky year as a player in the NBA started burning a hole in his pocket, so he approached his siblings with an idea: why don't they go into business together? After much discussion about the type of business they could successfully handle, they decided the restaurant business was the one. Now, keep in mind, this idea came from novices. All three older siblings had college degrees (the younger one was entering high school), but none had experience in the restaurant business, not even a summer job in a restaurant. But what they did have was a great deal of optimism.

With all the decisions in place, at least so they thought, they called Betty Jo and me to report their business venture. Being parents, we tried to advise them and point out the challenges they might face and the possible consequences. But like children everywhere, they chose not to listen. Instead, they were determined to give the restaurant business a whirl.

In the fall of 1974, D'Antoni's Yesteryear Restaurant in Myrtle Beach was scheduled to open, serving lunch and dinner. Betty Jo and I arrived in Myrtle Beach to lend support and helping hands. The restaurant was a friendly, cozy place that seated approximately ninety people. Two weeks before opening, the family sat down to plan the restaurant's menu. Since the restaurant had our family name, we felt that it should have some Italian sandwiches and dinners (a brilliant concept). We decided on pastrami sandwiches, meatball subs, and of course, spaghetti. Danny liked ham and cheese sandwiches, so that

went on the menu. Flying by the seat of our pants, we final-
ized the menu. Three days before opening, Danny made a sug-
gestion that maybe a run through on the menu items would
be good preparation. The idea was vetoed. Being a confident
bunch, everyone else thought it was a waste of time. We all
knew how to make a sandwich or dish out spaghetti.

Opening day arrived. The ensemble that gathered that day
would bring tears to a restaurateur's eyes. Betty Jo and two
of her sisters cooked the special of the day at Kathy's house,
which was two blocks away, and brought it to the restaurant.
Mike was the bartender. Not only did he not particularly care
to drink, but he had never even mixed a drink! The bar was
stocked with minibottles, and he had a bartender's guide to
drinks under the counter, so he was confident that he could
handle it. Danny was designated the short-order cook. His experience consisted of fixing a bowl of cold cereal for his kids.
Betty Jo was helping Danny in the kitchen, and Butch, a cousin
who was visiting for the week, agreed to be the dishwasher for
the opening day. Kathy, who had never waited tables before,
and Alice, Danny's wife, were waitresses. And Mark and I were
busboys. We were ready. Betty Jo had cautioned us not to be
disappointed if only a few people came in to eat on opening
day. Of course, that was fine with everybody because we felt a
slow start would help us work out any kinks. Or a better anal-
ogy would have been to help us moor knots.

At 11:00 AM on a sunny Thursday morning, D'Antoni's
Yesteryear opened for business. The first customer arrived
around 11:05. As the noon hour approached, the restaurant
was steadily getting busier, and our sense of calm was slowly
dissipating. At high noon, the entire work force of Myrtle
Beach decided to enjoy their lunch at D'Antoni's Yesteryear.
Within two hours, the staff of the tiny restaurant that seated
a maximum of 90 people tried to accommodate and feed 450
people. We estimate we successfully fed 175.

During the zany lunch hour, pandemonium reigned. A man
who sat at the bar ordered a Reuben. Mike was frantically

trying to find the ingredients for a Rueben in the bar manual. Danny had ham and cheese sandwiches strung from one end of the kitchen to the other. Betty Jo, who had prepared hundreds of meals, was nearing a stroke. Mark and I were running around trying to keep the tables bussed, and Kathy lost tickets, tables, and I think her mind. Opening day was a hysterically funny disaster. Surprisingly, we survived, and by the grace of God (there had to be divine intervention) the little restaurant became successful.

After a few months, the restaurant was running smoothly and efficiently. In designing the business venture, it was decided that Kathy would manage and everyone else would keep their respective jobs. However, it was agreed that Danny, who lived in Myrtle Beach, would relieve Kathy if she wanted a day off.

After the restaurant had been operating for several months, Betty Jo and I were visiting our children and thought it would be a good idea for Kathy to have a night off from working. She had spent long hours at the restaurant, and we thought it would be good for her to leave the business for a few hours and go to a movie with us. Danny agreed to take over as manager for the evening. Before leaving, Kathy asked Danny if he felt comfortable managing the restaurant. He answered with a typical sibling response: "I can do anything you can do!" Feeling that things were under control, Kathy left with us to see the movie.

After the movie, we went back to the restaurant. We walked past two customers sitting in a booth, laughing, talking, and having a good time and made our way to the bar where Danny was sitting.

"Did you have any trouble, Danny?" Kathy inquired. With a look that said that was a silly question, Danny replied everything was fine. After a few minutes, he stuck his hand close to our noses. It reeked of onions. "What have you been doing?" Kathy asked.

Danny smiled at us and replied smartly, "I told you I could handle it!" He paused a minute, and with a desire to impress us with his newfound knowledge, confidently stated, "I bet I know something you don't know! What's a Gibson?"

Laughing, Kathy said, "It's a martini with an onion in it. Why?"

Disappointed that Kathy knew the answer, Danny remarked, "How did you know that?"

"I work here, remember?" Kathy answered. Suddenly, a mental flashback reminded Kathy of the bar order for the next day. The bar was out of cocktail onions. Hesitantly, she stated, "Danny, we don't have any onions for Gibsons."

Danny proudly responded, "I know, but no problem, Kathy. I took care of it. I cut up some onions."

Flabbergasted, Kathy quietly screamed, "Danny, a Gibson has a marinated, special onion in it. You know, like an olive."

"Oh, my," Danny gulped. "You have to go over and talk with the couple sitting in the booth." He gestured to the people we had passed earlier.

With a panicked voice Kathy said, "What am I going to say to them, Danny?"

"I don't know, but you've got to talk to them," Danny pleaded. As she cautiously approached the booth, an unbelievable sight jumped into Kathy's view. Lying on the cocktail napkin next to the gentleman's so-called Gibson was a large, imposing onion ring.

"Sir," Kathy began apologetically, "I am so sorry about your drink. I'll be glad to get you another one, no charge."

"That's okay, lady," the gentleman laughingly replied. "It really doesn't taste that bad, and we haven't had this much fun since we left New York. However, we do have one problem. We don't know what to call the drink!"

Smiling, and looking at her brother with a superior sisterly attitude, Kathy quipped, "Call it? That's easy! You call it a 'dumb dago.' That's what you call it!"

The successful little restaurant was sold two years after it opened. A gentleman walked in one day and made an offer to buy. Kathy told the man that the restaurant was not for sale. He replied, "Lady, everything's for sale!" Thinking about his statement and agreeing, Kathy quickly calculated their investment in the restaurant, tripled the amount, and stated the sale price. Within two weeks, the restaurant was sold. And I am happy to say that my children left the restaurant business for good when they figured out it is not their niche in life. Education and basketball has proven to be their more successful callings.

Mark, who joined his other siblings a little later in life, is the youngest, but his bond with the rest of the kids is the same. The difference is that he has watched his siblings successes and misfortunes as they have traveled through life, and in doing so has developed a very cautious outlook as it pertains to folks outside the family circle. That caution came to fruition in the fall of '89 when Mark and new wife, Chelle, made plans to visit Mike in Rome, Italy, to watch Tracer Milan, Mike's professional basketball team, play Messaggero, the Rome team, who had just acquired former Duke player Danny Ferry. Mark and Chelle were traveling alone, and because they did not have a lot of traveling experience, Mike, at the urging of his wife, Laurel, warned them to be extremely careful with their luggage and money, as there was a high incidence of theft in the Rome area. Mark, who is naturally overly cautious, took the warning to heart.

They arrived at the hotel early in the afternoon. The cab driver unloaded the luggage and set their bags on the sidewalk as Mark counted out tip money. While Mark was giving the tip to the cab driver, a man, coming from the direction of the hotel, approached him and asked if he could help him with the luggage. Mark agreed. After he paid the cab driver and turned toward the luggage, Mark saw the man pick up the bags and run down the sidewalk away from the front of the hotel. Mark, who has watched one too many *Pink Panther* movies and was wearing his "be aware" button, knew he had been taken. After throwing a "Can you believe this?" look at Chelle, he bolted after the would-be thief.

Mark rounded the corner of the hotel in hot pursuit of the luggage bandit. Running down a narrow alley at high speed, Mark was closing the gap when the man suddenly stopped and entered a side elevator door. Mark reached the door just as it was closing. By placing both hands inside the doors and struggling against the weight of the closing doors, he managed to pull them apart. Mark, his luggage, and the thief were huddled together in a small elevator cubicle. Mark grabbed his bags, but the thief held on tight. They were arguing loudly in English and Italian, pulling back and forth on the luggage when the back door of the elevator suddenly opened. Pulling on the luggage with all the strength he could muster, Mark finally recaptured his bags as he stumbled out of the elevator. Relieved, he looked up. He could not believe his eyes. As reality set in, Mark's face turned crimson. He found himself standing in the hotel lobby and instantly realized, as well as did every other person in the busy lobby, that he had successfully apprehended the hotel's bell captain. This story is still a family favorite.

Being a father for over sixty years, I can confidently state that people who raise children should be eligible for the Purple Heart. There are many battles along the way, and serious wounds can occur. My advice is to provide your children with a good home life, to play games with them, and to teach them the value of having the will to win. When they don't win, teach them how to lose gracefully. As a society, we have lost the ability to have fun with kids when teaching them about competition and winning and losing. A common excuse today is that both parents work so it makes it difficult to have a good home life. Betty Jo and I both worked. We *had* to work in order to pay our bills, but we still had a great home life for our children.

On the subject of children, I must make this point. Over the past years, I have watched the evolution of children from playing in pickup games in their neighborhoods without adult interference to playing in highly structured supervised playground environments. I question why this has happened and what the value of it is for the children. Sitting in the bleachers to watch my grandchildren play in various sporting events, I've witnessed questionable acts from parents who scream at their kids and coaches and questionable acts from coaches who scream at the kids and refs. Kids react with fear and hesitation, and these actions bother me. It concerns me a great deal as I watch these little ones learn how to play in such a stressed arena. Organized sports are supposed to provide a safe and fun learning environment. What is going on in the minds of the adults that have caused the game to have the fun stripped from it? Through all the hundreds of little league baseball games, bitty league basketball games, bitty league football games, and others, I have yet to see one big league scout sitting in the stands looking for prospects.

Chapter Twelve:

The Baileys

Dad provided me with my moral and ethical fiber, but it was the Baileys, Betty Jo's family, who taught me how to treasure the journey. The Bailey's were a large family with ten children, all who married and settled within fifteen miles of each other, with the exception of Bernice, their third daughter, who moved to Ohio.

They were quite a family and were larger than life in exploits and sheer numbers. One colorful kinfolk who contributed to the family's rich history was the infamous cousin Devil Anse Hatfield, leader of the Hatfield clan who battled the McCoys. Although it was before Betty Jo's time, her sisters related the stories of Devil Anse hiding from both the McCoys and the Kentucky police officers at the Baileysville hotel owned by Grandfather Bailey. At dinner time, when he joined them at the table, Devil Anse was a menacing figure and the children were not allowed to speak during the meals.

In the Wyoming County communities of Mullens and Pineville, the Bailey family members were pillars of the community—lawyers, judges, elected public officials, and educators. My family was "legally" introduced to a member of

The Baileys (Front Row L-R Helen, Kate Bailey, Cal Bailey, Betty Jo Second Row (L-R) Kathleen, Bill, Garnet Lee, Bess, Sandy, and Theodore (not pictured Bernice and Allie)

the Bailey family fifteen years before I met Betty Jo. It was an introduction I'm sure Dad would rather not have happened.

It started out as a typical Monday, a school day. Di and I had already left for school, and Mom was about to send Olga on her way when the phone rang. It was Mom's sister who lived about three miles away, and she needed help because she was in labor. Mom told her she would be right there and told Olga to stay home and to babysit Anna, her younger sister.

Before noon, an unexpected visitor knocked at our front door. When Olga opened the door, she was surprised to find the school district's truant officer staring back at her. He loudly demanded to know why she was not in school. Frightened, Olga called Dad at the store and told him he had better come home, as there was a problem.

When Dad arrived, he was greeted by a crying Olga and a pompous truant officer. Dad explained the circumstances to the officer and the reason why Olga had stayed home, but the truant officer refused to listen. Instead, Dad was summoned to appear before the justice of the peace in the Barker's Ridge District and was fined $10.

Dad refused to pay. Not only did he think it was unfair, but the summons was issued from the Barker's Ridge District and he lived in the Slab Fork District. Dad hired an attorney to fight the charge. The story interested the editor of the local newspaper, and he wrote an editorial questioning the ethics of the magistrate who had issued the summons. In a newspaper interview, Dad was asked, "Why did you hire a lawyer as that will cost more than the fine?"

Dad replied, "I refuse to paya the fine. I am in *cerca di guistizia*" (seeking justice). Dad's attorney appealed the verdict and fine. The case was brought before the circuit court, and the appeal was heard by Judge R. D. Bailey, the brother of Cal Bailey and Betty Jo's uncle.

Judge Bailey overturned the lower court's decision and stated, "The squires should use better judgment and not burden this court with such cases." Judge R. D. Bailey became a very prominent political figure in West Virginia's history and was recognized at the national level. His retirement dinner attendees included members of the Kennedy family, and a federal dam, located in Baileysville, West Virginia, was named in his honor.

To give you a little insight into the Bailey clan, the day Betty Jo introduced me to her family members, the relatives present included the county school superintendent, the county sheriff, the county prosecutor, a postmaster, a business owner, two school principals, and four teachers. Needless to say, they were very politically influential in Wyoming County. This fact became apparent to three strangers who made the mistake of paying a felonious visit to one of the Bailey families who lived in the small town of Pineville, the county seat.

Crime in the town of Pineville usually involved moonshine makers, family disputes, and various misdemeanors. Major crimes and criminals were not a part of the small West Virginia town. But one spring day several years ago, the serenity of the area was shaken to the core.

A large, white house, hidden on the side of a mountain, was the scenic home site of Robert Bailey, the son of Judge R. D. Bailey and the current sitting West Virginia secretary of state and his wife, Jean. Although he held a public state office, he also was head of a local law firm. Approximately two hundred yards below their home was a trailer where their son, Bobby, lived alone.

On June 10, 1976, Robert, Jean, and a friend named Joe Lonker had just finished lunch when two men knocked on the front door. Robert answered the door and the men asked to talk with him about a possible divorce case. He invited the two men into the house, and they stepped through the door at the same moment Jean and Joe entered the foyer. Immediately, the men drew guns and ordered Robert, Jean, and Joe to move into the study, and then they demanded money. They reported that Bobby was being held hostage in his trailer and if they didn't return, Bobby would die.

The intruders were from Chicago and had cased the house for weeks after hearing rumors that large sums of money were kept in Robert's wall safe under the front stairs of the house. They instructed Joe and Jean to place their hands behind their backs as they proceeded to handcuff them. Jean asked to be handcuffed with her hands in front, explaining that she had severe arthritis, and they obliged. They would later regret this decision, as Jean had already thought of a plan. Once the handcuffs were in place, Robert was ordered to open the safe. In single file, with Robert in the lead followed by the two robbers and then Joe and Jean, they moved toward the stairs and the safe. As Robert began to open the safe, he heard the familiar squeak of the lid on the hi-fi that the group had just passed. He knew immediately what Jean was doing. They kept a loaded gun in the stereo, and Jean, like Betty Jo, was fearless. Both robbers were so intent on watching Robert open the safe that they did not notice Jean lifting the lid. In a flash, she grabbed the gun, stuck the revolver to the temple of the closest robber and demanded that both men drop their guns. The man who had Jean's gun aimed at his temple shakily stated, "I think I am going to faint."

Jean promptly responded, "If you faint, you'll be dead before you hit the floor."

The police arrived, and Bobby's rescue was successful. Jean had made it very clear to both men that if one hair on Bobby's head was harmed, they would never live to tell about it. She was very convincing.

The two men were taken to the county jail and Butch Goode, the prosecuting attorney, entered their cell. Looking at the three criminals, he shook his head in dismay and frankly stated, "You men have to be the dumbest SOBs that ever lived, or the unluckiest. You just tried to rob the secretary of state, in the town where his father is the judge, his uncle is the sheriff, half the town is related to him, and me, the prosecuting attorney, his cousin, is going to try you. You would have stood a better chance if you had tried to rob the Pope. Not everybody here knows the Pope, but everybody here does know Robert."

I'm sure these guys never forgot their visit to West Virginia and the Baileys. And they would be right: the Baileys were unforgettable. They were a special group. Their zeal for life and their expressive actions, good or bad, right or wrong, always made lasting impressions.

At each Bailey social gathering, everyone was genuinely excited to visit with everyone who attended, whether you were a newcomer or a family member. At some point during the visit, everyone would seek you out and ask, "How have you been? It's been a long time since we have talked. What's going on?"

Another might slyly quip, "Who let you in the door?"

It is an understatement to say that this family was not a quiet group. Keep in mind that these questions were being asked of all who were present, not as one single conversation taking place. The same words were repeated simultaneously in the small groups throughout the room. To illustrate, one day, a nephew visiting from Ohio walked into a family group who had gathered to see him. Listening to the noise of the many conversations, he stood in the midst of the relative-infested room and inquired loudly of the crowd, "Is anyone here talking to me?" The talking was immediately replaced by laughter, and without missing a beat, everyone returned to their original conversations. This reinforces the family credo that, regardless if you are a family member, local, visitor, or even a celebrity, you were not the story, only a loving part of it.

Regardless of the timbre of the inquiry, everyone was genuinely interested in you and wanted to talk. Questions about what was new in your life, how was work, and what were your children doing were interspersed with laughter, which was as abundant as the wonderful food heaped on large platters for all to enjoy. Small children darted in and out of the rooms but were never permitted to interrupt the affable tenor of the occasion. The love for life and each other encircled all and held you tight.

Kate, the mother of the brood, was the daughter of a traveling circuit judge. Accompanying her father and governess, Kate was sixteen when the group arrived in Baileysville for a court hearing. It did not take long for her to be noticed by a local young man named William Calhoun "Cal" Bailey, grandson of the founder of the town. When court was over and her father left town for another job, Kate was not in tow. Instead, she eloped the night before with the local young man, and needless to say, at that point, her dad was not enthralled with West Virginia. A petite woman with a brilliant mind, she remained in West Virginia for the rest of her life and ruled the roost as she raised her close-knit, loving family. The family grew from ten to fourteen when she opened her home and reared four grandchildren.

Betty Jo's Parents – Kate and Cal Bailey

Deeply religious, Kate, who had the heart of an angel, was the opposite of Cal, who was a lovable rascal. Family legend is that he would study the Bible just to argue with Kate. Church was an important part of their lives. Cal usually strayed from the fold during the week but faithfully attended church on Sunday. With his rich, bass voice, he directed the choir, selected the hymns, and led the congregation in song. One particular Sunday, the preacher delivered a hellfire damnation sermon on the evils of alcohol, ending the sermon with these words: "We should take all the bourbon that exists in the world and throw it in the river. All the vodka, gin, wine, and everything that contains the evil spirits of alcohol should be thrown in the river … Amen." After the sermon, Cal, who was known to enjoy a nip or two … or three, stood to announce the closing hymn. Looking out at the congregation with a twinkle in his eye, he loudly announced, "Turn to Hymn 136, 'Shall We Gather at the River.'"

Each Sunday, as long as Kate was alive, every child and their families was expected to eat Sunday dinner at her house. The schedule did not vary, as this day was reserved for Kate. During the rest of the week, her children often gathered often at each other's homes. The boisterous social gatherings included dinners, adult card games of setback and bridge, active children, and when weather permitted, picnics on the mountain, where their singing serenaded the valley nestled below. A family favorite, an old revival song, "Will the Circle Be Unbroken?" spoke to the true meaning of their family and was lovingly sung whenever an opportunity was available.

When at least four family members were together, you could be assured that within ten minutes a setback card game would happen. Many hours were spent around a card table going for the win, coveting the quarter ante, and defending one's pride.

It is family knowledge that a few of the trusted group seemed to be luckier than others in setback, so their opponents had to watch them and their cards carefully. In his will, Bill, my brother-in-law, who kept score and usually won, left his setback scoring pencil to his sister Garnet Lee, assuring her that over time it would increase her winnings.

During one heated battle of setback, Cousin Sandy raised the ire of Betty Jo and brothers-in-law Paul and Pete with his suspicious wins. Sandy, trying to keep the atmosphere congenial, readily assured them that he had not cheated since he had been "saved." The play continued and after Sandy won the next three games, Betty Jo looked at him and quietly remarked, "I think it's time for another baptism."

Serious Business

Each member of the Bailey family was a memorable, love-able, character, unique in a style of his or her own. All were extroverted, and they lovingly taught this shy Italian boy how to enjoy life. When I first met them, I was a bit overwhelmed, but they quickly put me at ease. I soon learned that newcomers were always welcome, but if you couldn't take the ribbing that this family loved to dish out, then you definitely had married into the wrong group.

No family event was passive, as laughter, games, and song ruled the day. Even funerals were a celebration for this vibrant loving family as they remembered the one who had left the tight group through humorous stories. Today, I am the only surviving member of the immediate Bailey clan, but I am witness to the fact that the Bailey's lived life to its fullest through deep, respectful love, and constant and boisterous laughter. All were lively spirits who were full of song. The ride they gave me could not have been better.

Scenes from Betty Jo's Kitchen

Scenes from Betty Jo's Kitchen

Scenes from Betty Jo's Kitchen

Scenes from Betty Jo's Kitchen

Chapter Thirteen:

Coaching

If I had to choose a time in my life when I was the happiest, it would be during my coaching years. Nothing can compare to the excitement of the game and the sheer joy of working with young people and assisting them as they grew to adulthood. Many of my players return to visit me in Mullens, and it is wonderful to observe how these young men have grown and prospered. Our conversation centers around their life experiences, and we reminisce about the high school basketball games, our wins, and our losses. A few of these players are now basketball coaches themselves, and we spend time discussing techniques and coaching philosophies. I guess because of all the years of playing, coaching, and now watching the game of basketball, they are interested in my thoughts on coaching.

The joy of coaching is definitely magnified by winning. But the reality of coaching is that you will experience losses, and because you compete publicly, the losses are there for others to comment on. In my opinion, there are few things harder to accept than a loss where every fiber in your body was laid on the line in the competition and the result was not in your favor. But even worse is to suffer an unfair loss that life sometimes hands you. Even though we have been fortunate in the coaching and playing venues, the D'Antoni family has had their share of both types of losses.

I have also noticed that in sports, as in life, sometimes losing is perceived as failing. They are totally different. Losing is an occurrence that creates a response within an individual. The response to losing will determine if it is just an occurrence or if it is failure.

Because of certain losses, my children and my teams at times could have given up on their dreams. But they didn't. Each time they were knocked down, they got back up—and they got up with fire in their bellies. Because of their tenacity, their losses were eventually turned into victories. Life is not always fair, but in my experiences over time, it does reward the relentless.

To cultivate the proper attitudes and positive responses to winning and losing, my approach to coaching basketball is to develop the team as a family. A family where each member knows his importance and the expectations required of him, but which supports the individual in overcoming individual losses.

As a coach and the head of the family, it was important to me to never embarrass my ballplayers. If a player made a mistake during a ball game, he would not be pulled out immediately. After a couple of plays had ensued, I then took the player out of the game. He would sit next to me on the bench while I explained what he did wrong.

Now, if a player suddenly decided he was not part of the whole but was the whole part, then a different approach was used. This happened during a game where one of my players began cherry-picking. For those who aren't familiar with basketball jargon, cherry-picking is when a player hangs around the half-court line and watches the other members of the team do the hard work on defense and rebounding. Once the team secures the rebound, then the player who is cherry-picking conveniently waits for the rebounder to throw him the ball so he can score the points and get the publicity. As this particular game progressed, it became obvious that one of my players was cherry-picking and not playing team defense. My point guard began to complain, so I instructed him to keep the ball away from the cherry-picker. Under no circumstances was he to get the ball. It wasn't long before the message became clear. Within a few plays, the cherry-picker understood that this was not acceptable behavior and returned to team play. Lessons that are learned from the consequences of personal actions make more of an impact on players than verbal reprimands.

As to the style of basketball I like my teams to play, it is unequivocally the up-tempo style. There are continuous discussions surrounding which is the best ball game pace, the bum-and-grind tempo or the up-tempo grind. Bump-and-grind tempo is all about control. A bump-and-grind defense gives the control to the coach. In an up-tempo, free-flowing ball club, the control is passed to the players and the coach becomes a facilitator. Many coaches are not comfortable in a facilitating role. But the real beauty of basketball is only witnessed with an up-tempo style of play. Nothing is more exciting and compelling than watching a team as they execute the proper skills and winning maneuvers at a high energy level and a rapid pace. A team that possesses the excellent physical conditioning required for the up-tempo game pace and is led by a point guard—a maestro—who ably conducts the orchestrated performances night after night, will quickly establish themselves as winners.

The point guard is the key to developing a team of this level. The guard must be a player who sees the whole floor, understands the flow of the game, and makes accurate and instantaneous decisions. Simply stated, a point guard must have a high basketball IQ. Consequently, teams with a mediocre point guard have a mediocre team; teams with outstanding point guards have outstanding teams. A majority of practice time with my teams was spent developing point guards, and it is no coincidence that all three of my boys were point guards. Throughout my career, I was fortunate to develop good-to-outstanding point guards, and because of them, I was a successful coach.

My son Danny followed in my career footsteps to coach high school basketball at Socastee High School in South Carolina. A successful high school coach with over five hundred wins, Danny's teams in South Carolina incorporated the up-tempo pace. His teams' successes helped Danny secure college basketball scholarships for hundreds of student athletes. Additionally, he also founded and directed the Beach Ball Classic, named the number one holiday high school basketball tournament in America. Current NBA players who played in the tournament include Kobe Bryant, Kevin Garnett, and Jason Kidd.

But more importantly, the significance of the Beach Ball Classic superseded the game. It created a community of family and an event that continues to be celebrated even today.

In Italy and in Phoenix, Mike continued the coaching philosophy, perfecting the up-tempo game. As a result, he won Italian championships and almost won an NBA championship. Mike became one of the premier coaches in Europe and the NBA and was selected NBA Coach of the Year in 2005. Even though the tempo was fast, Mike's 2005–06 Phoenix team was ranked sixth in defense in the league. The team as a whole had an above-average basketball IQ, but injuries and flawed circumstances kept the championships from happening. I am certain a championship will happen for one of Mike's team. Hopefully, it will be New York.

Chapter Fourteen:

Mullens, West Virginia—
My Home Town

The sense of family not only works for a team, but its synergy creates an even larger family unit within the community. This happened in the tiny West Virginia town of Mullens. It was an extraordinary place, and in the 1950s, its townspeople helped mold a special time in history. I wonder if my dad's superstitious nature sensed out the unique qualities of this small town when he made the decision to move to Mullens thirty years before.

Mullens is nestled between two large mountains in southern Appalachia. The population in the 1950s was approximately five thousand people. The town is built within a long narrow valley that winds west-to-south for approximately two or three miles. Starting in the middle of the downtown business area and continuing to the south end of Mullens, the residential community stretches up one side of a mountain. Directly across the valley on the other side runs the Guyandotte River, flanked by railroad tracks and another mountain.

The makeup of the community, of the people who worked and lived there, created a Mayberry-esque way of life that was uncharacteristically interwoven with a cosmopolitan culture. It was a community neighborhood where folks flowed in and out of each other's homes with ease and familiarity and the local conversations centered on national topics, good books, and politics.

Dinner theaters existed, political teas for high-ranking officials took place, and shop owners traveled to New York to buy the latest fashions. There was no crime, the doors were open and unlocked, and children played throughout the town from morning to night. No one worried about the children because they had parents at home and they had community parents who watched out for them. My children learned very early that if they did anything wrong while they were away from home, we would know about it before they returned.

Mullens was the personification of American values and life, and the young people who grew up there had a childhood that money could not purchase; they were wealthy far beyond the bank account. Danny, my son, once remarked about his childhood, "We didn't have to go outside the city limits. We had everything we needed or wanted in Mullens."

School was the vehicle that united the community. Parents, whether they were railroaders, miners, teachers, or businessmen, worked together to provide the support structure necessary to develop a successful young person.

The arena that allowed the town to come together to celebrate as a family was sports. Our basketball team's victories translated into community victories. This type of victory goes beyond a single person or coach and transcends into the greatest victory of all—where everyone in the family shares in the wins and losses.

The town and its citizens gave hours of their personal time to work with young folks in whatever venue they selected. Playgrounds were strategically placed throughout the town, and lights for night basketball or tennis were purchased. Consequently, during the summer, playgrounds were full of young people, and pickup basketball games were abundant.

I ran the summer league basketball program for ten years, and we had some great basketball players from Mullens who played at the college and pro levels. I firmly believe the extra time these kids spent outdoors playing pickup games built their confidence and skill levels and played a major role in their athletic successes when they were older.

It was not just the sports arena where our children succeeded. Each child developed an innate feeling that they were worthy of love and riches and could do anything they aspired to do. As a result, this small town boasts of its children becoming doctors, lawyers, CEOs of major businesses, educators, and college presidents. Talk with anyone who grew up in Mullens during this time and they will recall for hours about the town, its people, and how thankful they are to have grown up there. I wish someone would research the lives of folks who were raised in Mullens during the 1950s and 1960s and compare their accomplishments to those of people from other towns across the nation. I think it would be an incredible statistic.

Just as they exhibited throughout my lifetime, the people of Mullens still work diligently to promote the family both within the whole unit of the town and in the smaller unit of single families. In the spring of 2009, the Mullens Chamber of Commerce held a celebration for the town, "A Night with the D'Antoni's." The focus was to celebrate the high accomplishments of Mike and Danny, but in so doing it recognized the value and accomplishment of the whole family within the community. Danny remarked, "What was wonderful about the event was that we (the family) had the distinct feeling that even if Mike and I were not coaches for the New York Knicks, the townspeople would still be happy to see us." The great thing about his comment—it was true.

Chapter Fifteen:

Journey to Destiny

Prior to the 1950s, we always had a good basketball team, but we never were able to make it to the state tournaments. A major reason for this was that our gym was not regulation size and doubled as an auditorium for the high school. The lack of size restricted us from practicing as we should, and because it could only seated three hundred people, the team was not experienced with playing in front of the big crowds we encountered at away games.

That all changed in the '50s. By then, Mullens was a bustling little town. On Saturday nights, it was hard to drive through the downtown area because of all the people. Betty Jo loved to park our car in the downtown area and just people watch. It was the fabulous fifties, and life was good.

The coaching situation was also good because this time period began the great winning tradition for the basketball program at Mullens High School.

I was blessed to be at the beginning of the tradition that continued under the tutelage of coaches such as Abe Wyatt, Sonny Phillips, Norm Brewer, Don Stover, Don Nuchols, and Gene Reid, until school consolidation in 2004. I was very fortunate to have had Abe Wyatt, a proven winner, as my assistant

Mullens High School

coach. To be able to coach the caliber of basketball players and young men who came through the doors of Mullens High School was also a blessing. Not only were these young men eager to learn and dedicated to the sport of basketball, they were upstanding individuals from families in Mullens where children were taught respect for others, especially for their teachers and coaches. Parents gave them the ability to develop the skills to work hard in their endeavors and to persevere in tough times. Our success was created and sustained by the quality of the entire community.

At the beginning of our 1950 season, we took a three-game road trip, which was an uncommon practice for high school basketball teams at that time. West Virginia roads were two lanes, some paved and some not, and steep mountains had to be crossed when teams traveled from town to town. To reach Huntington, West Virginia from Mullens during the '50s, it took our team four to five hours depending on coal truck traffic. For comparison, today it is about two hours and twenty minutes. Our first game of the trip was against Vinson High School in Huntington. Next stop was Ceredo Kenova High School, located on the outskirts of Huntington, and before

Coaches – L-R Abe White, Lewis D'Antoni, Jim Elwood

our return to Mullens, the last stop was Logan High School in Logan, West Virginia. Our first game was victorious, as we won 51–47, and it was not as close against Ceredo Kenova, as we won 44–35.

Arriving in Logan, we were feeling rather good about our abilities. Like many other schools throughout the state, the gymnasium was not part of the school complex. Instead, the game was held in the Moose Lodge gymnasium. To get to the court, our team had to walk through a room where lodge members were smoking, drinking, and playing poker. I vividly remember lots of smoke. All of us held our breaths, trying not to breathe the air as we passed through the room on our way to the gym. It was an intimidating stroll through this hazy, odorous room.

The game did not start off going very well for us. As a matter of fact, Logan was beating us rather handily. Not only were our shots not falling, but we were not playing with

Coach D'Antoni

any type of energy or determination. At the beginning of the fourth quarter, Logan was leading by eighteen points. For some reason, the Logan coach, who was assured that he had the win in hand, took several of his regulars out of the game and sent them to the locker room to shower. After they left the court, we started to make a run, slowly getting back into the game. In a short amount of time, we were within eight points. Panicking, the Logan coach sent for his starters in the locker room. Within minutes, the starting ballplayers that had left the floor were running back to the bench. Their hair was wet from the interrupted shower, and they were busy pulling and tugging on their uniforms. It was a very funny sight. Their return to the game, however, was to no avail. Our boys with dry hair and intact uniforms defeated Logan 53–51, leaving us with a perfect three-game road trip. The long ride home over the mountains seemed much shorter that night.

In 1950, the county built a new gym for Mullens High School, and we were eyeing the state tournaments for the first time in the history of the school. Unlike today with schools divided into classifications based on school enrollment, the state of West Virginia did not have the various class sections for sports in the '50s. There was only one classification regardless of the school population. This meant Mullens, a very small school, had to compete against much larger schools in the state. In the early '60s, the Commission for Secondary School Activities established new guidelines, with three classifications for schools, and Mullens began competing against schools their own size. Consequently, the entire '50s basketball era in Mullens was played in a David versus Goliath environment. That is why in 1950, when Mullens had a good shot at cracking the state tournament level, there was so much excitement. Unfortunately, the run to the state playoffs that year came to an abrupt halt at the regional playoff finals, one game away from the state tournament.

In the first round of the regional, Denny Lowe, my center whose family had moved to Mullens so he could play basketball, got tangled up with Princeton's big center. After they pulled the two apart, Denny came out of the tussle with a sprained knee. We were able to win the game, but we had to face Big Creek High School in the final. Their basketball team had a big center named Stretch Willis, and sadly, our center had a bad knee and was unable to play. The game was very exciting, and when the buzzer ended regulation play, the score was tied. As the buzzer sounded again, ending the first overtime, the score was still tied. With twenty seconds left in the second overtime, we were down one point. My player was at the line shooting two shots. He missed both foul shots, and we lost the game to Big Creek. Our first trip to the state tournament was not to be that year.

Finally, we made it to the state tournament in 1951 with a team record of 20-4. The excitement was high as we left Mullens for the state tournament site, Morgantown, West Virginia. Our first game in the tournament was against Morgantown High School. The team was coached by Charlie Huggins, whose son Bob is now the head coach at West Virginia University. After arriving at the field house, I sent my team to the dressing rooms to get ready. I noticed a few of them looked a little peaked, but I attributed it to nerves.

A few minutes later, I entered our dressing room. My players were sitting on the benches with heads hanging and nobody dressed. My team manager ran up to me, excited and out of breath as he blurted out, "Coach, we forgot to pack the uniforms." My heart sunk. Racking my brain for a solution, I turned to Gordon Thorn, the tournament host assigned to our team. He was one of my former players and was a freshman at West Virginia University. His job was to take care of our needs, and, boy, did I ever have a need! He came up with a solution. He told me he would be right back. In a very short time, Gordon returned carrying a set of WVU's basketball uniforms. Our team was quite a sight. Trying to fit high school players into college-sized uniforms was not easy, but we did the best we could.

Adding to the problem was the fact that several of my players, who were queasy before the game, became worse. By halftime, five of my players were lying on the benches with upset stomachs and other flu-like symptoms. We finished the game but lost our first state tournament endeavor 51-58. Remembering back to that game, I know we would have played much better if we had been able to keep our basketball shorts up and our food down.

For the second time in as many years, we advanced to the state basketball tournament in 1952 with a season record of 20-3. Our leading scorer that season was Kenneth Coleman, had been dropped from the Welch High School basketball team. When state trooper Bob Tabscott found out about it, he persuaded Coleman's parents to move to Itmann, a small coal camp outside of Mullens. He not only arranged for the Coleman family to move, he found them a house. Kenneth was our tallest player at six-four, but he was unable to help us secure a state title. We lost in the first round of the state basketball tournament to Fairmont West, coached by Biz Dawson.

The 1953 basketball season was a season of contradictions. It was both my first losing season at Mullens High School and the foundation for the eventual win of a state championship. Our season record was 9–13, and toward the end of the season, I revamped my team by inserting sophomores Bob Tabscott, Terry Penn, and David Miller into the starting lineup. The experience they gained during this year proved vital for the upcoming seasons in 1954 and 1955.

The 1954 basketball team was tremendous. Our record was 25–2. During the season, we played the Woodrow Wilson Flying Eagles, our biggest rivals, twice. Coached by Gerome Van Meter, a phenomenal high school coach, the team represented Woodrow Wilson High School, which had an enrollment that was three times as large as Mullens.

Our rivalry over a five-year span was incredible. During this timeframe, we played Beckley's team, Woodrow Wilson, twenty-eight times, with Beckley winning fifteen and Mullens thirteen. At one point in the series, we had won six straight game, four by one point. After the fourth game of losing by one point, Coach Van Meter approached me and mumbled, "Gosh darn it, D'Antoni. If you are going to beat me, at least do it by more than one point." Being the nice guy that I was, I respected his wishes, and that year we won both regular season games against them by scores of 64–53 and 53–49.

During the '54 season, our games against Beckley were very testy. Beckley had an outstanding player by the name of Dwayne Wingler. He may have been one of the finest ballplayers I ever coached against, but his temperament created

Great Rivals – D'Antoni and VanMeter

problems for himself, his team, and us. Our first regular season game against Beckley that year was played on their home court in the recreation center. As usual, the game was close, with the lead changing back and forth. Mullens was ahead with one minute and thirty seconds to play, and Vernon Hurt, my point guard, was freezing the ball, dribbling it up and down the sidelines. Wingler, who was guarding someone else, decided to take the game into his own hands. He left his man and began running toward Vernon. On his approach, he threw a full football body block on Vernon, knocking him two rows up in the bleachers, which were packed with fans watching the ball game. Wingler fouled out, and Vernon, who was injured, had to leave the game. Mullens, however, went on to win the game.

As a result of the blatant foul, Vernon had to sit out the next regular season game because of bruised ribs. The Mullens fans, coaches, and players were extremely upset. The feelings grew even stronger as the next Beckley versus Mullens game approached. It is unbelievable to me that no punitive action was taken against Wingler. Even the Beckley newspapers ignored the incident. It was as if nothing had happened in the game. If a player on my team had conducted themselves in such a thug-like manner, they would have been suspended from the team and from school for at least two games. People in the town of Mullens were outraged.

The return game was played in Mullens a couple of months later in February. Security for the games was doubled, with state police highly visible throughout the gym. Spectators began to arrive early and filled the gym to capacity an hour before the game began. To accommodate the overflow crowd, spectators were directed to the auditorium, where they could listen to the game's broadcast on the radio. Finally, the Beckley team bus arrived at the front of the gym, and people trying to get into the game turned to glare at the Beckley basketball players and their coaches as they filed off the bus. Everyone was trying to get a look at Wingler, and angry eyes searched the Beckley unit entering the gym. No one could spot Wingler. Where was he? Where was the dirty ballplayer who didn't have a right to be on the same floor as our Mullens players? He was nowhere to be seen. Word quickly spread that Coach Van Meter had left Wingler at home because he was afraid for his safety. Which was ridiculous. Folks in Mullens and our team may have been angry over the incident, but no one would have acted outside of the law for revenge. The town of Mullens and the basketball team had a higher level of morality and character than what was shown to us.

To this day, the incident still haunts me with agitating thoughts. Although Mullens won the game that night, by 78–69, our opportunity to neutralize our frustrations and anger was denied. The air had been deflated out of a huge balloon, and there was nothing to show for it. It definitely affected me and my team's psyche and hung over us as a large gloomy cloud throughout the year.

The successful season ended, and the town of Mullens was once again buzzing with excitement as the state tournament approached. With only two losses during the season, the expectations were high. The first round in the state tournament was against Huntington East, a school with an enrollment four times our size. What a great game it was! East had an eight-point lead with two minutes to play. Our full-court pressure finally got to them, and we outscored them thirteen to three in the final minutes of the game. We won by 74–70

Our next tournament game was against Stonewall Jackson, another larger school that was favored to win the 1954 state tournament. On our way to the tournament site in Morgantown, we stopped at Buckhannon, West Virginia to practice. After our practice was over, Stonewall Jackson's team burst onto the floor. An impressive sight, they looked more like a college team than a high school one. With excellent size and beautiful uniforms, they looked incredible. Our nerves began to show a little, especially the coaches'.

Abe and I stayed up all night working on a game plan to defeat Stonewall Jackson. Our final decision was to implement a full-court man-to-man defense. Our offense was mainly using a pick-and-roll with Vernon Hurt, our point guard, and W. D. Akers, our power forward. Stonewall could not stop us. To everyone's surprise, we were leading at half time, 42–33. Against all odds, we went on to win the game, 79–67. In my opinion, we beat the best team in the tournament that night, a team with three outstanding players who received college scholarships from major 1A division schools—Jim Loughtin to Ohio State, Bobby Joe Smith to West Virginia University, and John Hemmings to Virginia Tech.

Getting out of bed the next day, we began to realize where we were and what we had accomplished. Everything began to settle in, the nerves, the excitement, and the awe. Here we were, a team from the small town of Mullens, playing in the finals for the state high school basketball championship. Our small school with less than six hundred students was competing against West Virginia's largest schools, and we were in the finals. The night before the final game, we received a 1,303 word telegram from the town of Mullens that wished us luck in the championship game. To send a telegram of this magnitude was unprecedented in that day, as it cost $49.30, a very large sum.

Good Luck Telegram

Finally, the day arrived for the 1954 state high school basketball finals. And wouldn't you know it? We had to meet Beckley High School and Wingler, our archrivals. They advanced to the final round by narrowly beating Morgantown High School in a last-second shot, and here we were, face-to-face again.

The starting tip-off hit the air, and the championship game was underway. Throughout the game, we had difficulty finding our rhythm. Our timing was not to our advantage, as we had played hard-fought games for two straight nights against great opponents. Unfortunately, Wingler was having a great game, and it seemed to me that we were more preoccupied with what Wingler was doing during the game rather than running our game plan. Thinking back, I think we just ran out of gas. Plus, I feel that if Wingler had shown up in Mullens to play in the final regular season game, we would have gotten over our frustration with him and his team and our focus in the title game would have been more on winning the title and less on him. The game ended with Mullens losing, 66–84.

The mood on the bus the next day was very subdued. Our spirits were low, and no one was talking. We had lost the state championship game. No one wanted to believe it or talk about it. As we approached Mullens, we heard faint sounds like people singing. The closer we got to town, the louder the singing became. As we rounded a curve about four miles outside of the city limits, we were stopped by the city police and directed to find places to stand or sit along the top and sides of the city fire truck. As the fire truck carrying our entire team came closer to Mullens, the singing became louder and louder until finally we could see why. Hundreds of people lined the route into Mullens. Over four hundred cars had moved in behind and in front of the fire truck, providing a celebratory caravan to the high school. Folks were singing, waving, and shouting our school song, "On you Rebels." It was a sight to behold. Everyone in town was celebrating our team. One of my players turned to me and asked, "We did lose, right?"

Smiling, I replied, "Yes, but only the game."

It was a memorable time for my team, for me, and for the community. Each player and coach spoke to the crowd that had gathered at the high school. We vowed that next year our team would play again in the finals and the championship trophy would be riding with us when we returned to Mullens.

After a long off-season, the 1955 basketball season finally began, and the Mullens High School basketball program was pushing toward its promised destination. The year 1955 is often referred to in Mullens as *the* year that Mullens High School's basketball team, a little upshot of a school, took on the big boys across the state and dominated the courts. Our basketball team breezed through the season, ending with a 25-2 record.

We entered the state tournament in Huntington in March, confident this was our year. My team had hopes they would leave Huntington and return to Mullens as the West Virginia high school boys basketball champions. It was my job to make it happened.

The first game of the playoffs was against Wheeling High School. They had lost only one regular season game, and we beat them by twenty points. Our confidence was soaring.

The next game was against Keyser High School. We were in the locker room getting dressed for the game when my manager rushed in and excitedly said to me, "Coach, T and David," who were my two starting guards, "can't get into the game. They are at the door, but the ticket taker won't let them in. They told me to tell you and have you come to the front of the arena to vouch for them."

Incredulous, I looked at the nervous manager and said, "I gave them their tickets for the game before we got to the arena. What did they do with them?"

"I don't know, they just told me to come get you."

"Well, you go back and tell them we go on the floor in ten minutes and they better be there and in uniform.

"But Coach," the manager pleaded, "how are they going to get in?"

I shook my head in irritation and said, "They'll just have to figure it out for themselves." The nervous team manager looked at me in disbelief, obviously thinking, *Doesn't Coach realize those are two of the main guys on the team, and we're playing in the semifinals of the state tournament?*

I turned away from the manager and took a deep breath to calm my nerves. Kids! The most important day of their young lives, and they had either given away their tickets or sold them. Well, either way, they needed to learn a lesson. They got themselves into the mess, and they could get themselves out of it. I just prayed that the whole team wouldn't have to pay for their careless antics. As we ran through the locker room doors and onto the court, the last two guys running onto the court were T and David. I never asked them what they did with the tickets or how they got in, and to this day, I have no clue. Thank goodness we won the game easily. The next game was Saturday night, the state basketball finals.

Chapter Sixteen:

Encountering Destiny

March, 25, 1955. This day would be like no other in the history of the town. Newspapers thudded as they landed on the front porches in Mullens, and the early risers, those who had not traveled to the games, read the news. The headlines screamed: MULLENS HIGH SCHOOL REBELS PITTED AGAINST HUNTINGTON HIGH SCHOOL PONY EXPRESS—TONIGHT. It was the day of the finals, and the town of Mullens was energized. Conversations at the barber shop, grocery stores, filling stations, and restaurants focused on one subject: the game. This was *it*.

Huntington High had an outstanding basketball player by the name of Leo Byrd, who went on to be a star at Marshall University. Leo averaged thirty points a game during the regular season. A prolific scorer and defender, he was the total package. In a hotel room with Abe, my assistant, we laid out the defensive strategy for our game against Huntington High. Using pennies, I designed what is commonly known today as a box-and-one. I put Gordon Brooks, my best defender, in the one slot and would have him shadow Byrd the entire time. He was not to leave him for a minute, to get in his hip pocket and ride. The rest of the team would be in a zone defense.

The next day, game time had arrived. Taking a deep breath and calming my nerves, my team (all of them this time), Coach Wyatt, and I entered the doors of the site of the championship game, Huntington Memorial Field House. We had the chance to make high school sports history. Unknown to me at the time, I would enter these doors numerous times years later to watch Danny and Mike as they made their own history.

The game plan was set. Earlier, as I scouted Huntington High and Byrd, I noticed that Byrd scored many of his points off his own rebounds. Once he shot the ball, he immediately followed his shot to the basket, putting himself in a good rebounding position for his missed shots. Then he would shoot the ball back up on the boards and score. So I pulled Gordon, who was to guard Leo Byrd, aside and told him to put his body between him and the basket every time Leo shot the ball. I instructed him to be in front of Byrd when he followed his shot to the basket. It worked to perfection. At the end of the third quarter, we had outscored Huntington High by thirty points. In the fourth quarter, I began to substitute, making certain all my players got in the game. When the game ended, we had won by a score of 87–74. It was the first state basketball championship for Mullens High School. In the game, Leo Byrd had been held to fourteen points until we started substituting freely in the fourth quarter. Our promise to the people of Mullens was fulfilled. We were West Virginia high school basketball champions!

Our team had the opportunity to set all kinds of state records that night if I had left the starters in for the fourth quarter. But in my mind, records are made to be broken, but playing in a state championship game lasts a lifetime. Every player on our team played in the championship game that night, and all have lifetime memories.

My '55 team placed four players as starters on the all-tournament team: W. D. Akers, a great rebounder, scorer, and defensive player; Terry Penn, a great point guard and ball handler; Bob Tabscott, a prolific scorer with a great touch; and

Dave Miller, a great defender and scorer. It was the first time this had happened in the forty-two-year history of the event. Even though Gordon Brooks, the player that held Byrd down in the game, did not make the all-tournament team, he definitely made my all-tournament list—he played a major role in our championship game win.

The next morning, the headlines in the papers across the state boldly reported MULLENS REBELS CAGED THE BYRD. And, so we did. We began our trip home. This year the atmosphere on the bus ride back home was different. Euphoria ruled the day. Laughter and loud voices filled the air. We stopped at Shoney's Big Boy restaurant in Charleston, and as a reward for their accomplishment, each player was allowed to order two Big Boy Hamburgers, one more than was the custom, and a drink.

As we approached the city limits, an incredible sight greeted us. The people in Mullens had turned out in huge numbers, lining the route to the high school with cheering fans. The high school grounds were engulfed. Over two thousand people, students, parents, and townspeople were cheering loudly for the returning champs. Fifty-four years later, that day is as crystal clear in my mind as it was the day it happened. No one thought a team from a small community like Mullens could compete against the larger schools in the state, much less win a state championship. It just wasn't possible. But we did it. What a miraculous moment in time.

400-Car Motorcade Escorts Team Home

Champ Rebels Given Big Welcome by Town Folks

MULLENS (RNS) — Basketball-happy Wyoming countians turned out enmasse yesterday to welcome the Class A state champion, Mullens high school Rebels, on their return home from a precedent-setting tournament engagement. History was regarded as the newly-crowned champs of the West Virginia hardwood rolled into Mullens at the head of 400-car, police-escorted caravan to receive the cheers and tumultous ovations of hundreds.

Never before had a basketball team returned to the "Hills o Wyoming" with the glory an recognition earned by the 195 Rebel squad in three days at Hunt ington.

It was a momentous occasion one that Mullens townspeople and many of their neighbors were rightfully proud of. And they did much to show it.

Crowds lined the streets and the cavalcade of cars and fire truck with horns and sirens blaring away pulled into town to be joined by the Mullens high school band and more vehicles.

Shop and locomotive whistles added to the noise.

Signs reading "Welcome Home Champs," "We're Proud of You," "Yea Blue, Yea Gray," etc., plus rolls on rolls of crepe paper adorned the pavement, cars, store fronts and theater marquees.

Mayor Woodrow W. Cook, unquestionably one of Mullens High's proudest alumni, had called ahead

TRIUMPHAL ENTRY — The Wyoming County fire truck carrying Coach Lewis D'Antoni and the state basketball champion Mullens Rebel players arrives in Mullens at the head of a 400-car procession to be greeted by exuberant townspeople celebrating the Wyoming County school's first state basketball championship. The celebration lasted over two hours.

Hoping for Victory

Mullens 1955 State Basketball Championship Team
1st Row L-R Bob Short, Terry Penn, Ronnie Cook, Bob
Tabscott, Wilbur Blankenship, Willie Akers, Gordon Brooks,
Dave Miller
2nd Row L-R Asst. Coach T.C. Wyatt, Rick Tolley, Roy Stover,
Hampton Hoge (mgr.), Gene Hoge, Jimmy Greene

Celebration Party

**Lewis D'Antoni in the Mullens High School Gymnasium
setting with the 1955 Championship Trophy**

BECKLEY POST-HERALD, BECKLEY, W. VA., TUESDAY MORNING, MARCH 22, 1955

ELATED BASKETBALL FANS turned out in large numbers to form | all sections of Wyoming County. More vehicles and hundreds of peo-
400-car, police-escorted caravan to usher home the Class A State | ple afoot joined the cavalcade on its arrival in Mullens. Allowing
Champion Mullens High School Team on its triumphant return from | 25 feet for each vehicle, the caravan would have stretched almost
Huntington Sunday. The reception, part of the ceremony planned for | two miles.
the occasion, was organized by boosters of the Rebel Squad from |

Interview Time

Welcome Home Parade

Chapter Seventeen:

Encore Season

The 1956 season began with Willie Akers as the lone returning starter, but we had three good players who stepped up to the challenge and made the starting team: Wilbur Blankenship, Ronnie Cook, and Gene Miller. Plus, an unexpected basketball player showed up in the halls of Mullens High School that year.

During my coaching tenure, the average height of our basketball players was less than six feet. So, during the 1956 school year when Claire Rowe, six-six and about 230 pounds, enrolled at Mullens High School, he made quite an impression. I am not sure how or why Claire came to Mullens. I do know that he walked across the mountain through Measle Creek, a small community about seven miles from Mullens, and ended up at Mullens High School one morning. Our high school principal found Claire roaming the halls of the high school. He asked Claire what he wanted. Claire responded, "I want to go to school." The principal enrolled him in classes, gave him a place to sleep at the school, and hired him to do odd jobs around the campus so he could earn a little money. When I saw Claire in the halls, I got excited. I asked Claire if he had ever played basketball. He told me no and that he didn't know anything about the game. So I immediately gave him a basket-ball and told him to go to the gym and play around with the ball, dribble, shoot at the baskets in his spare time, just to get familiar with handling the ball. Claire agreed.

Claire was enrolled for classes at the high school in the mornings. In the afternoons, he traveled to Pineville to a county vocational school that served the three high schools in the area. Jesse Houck was one of my brother-in-laws and was also the principal of Pineville High School, a major rival of Mullens High School. He saw Claire at the vocational school and convinced him to change schools and enroll at Pineville High School. He even drove him to the school in his personal car. When the principal from Mullens High School heard what had happened, he jumped in his car and drove to Pineville High School, where he found Claire and bought him back to Mullens.

Claire was a member of my '56 team, and these young men were a group of overachievers. All but Claire had tasted the success of a state championship, and they wanted it again. Our season record was twenty-two wins and four losses and, again, we were primed and ready to repeat the championship.

As fate would have it, we were matched in the first round against our nemesis, the Beckley Flying Eagles. This year, they had one of their greatest teams in school history and were led by Howard Hurt, an outstanding point guard who went on to play for Duke Blue Devils. They had defeated us twice, decisively, during the regular season. Only one loss marred Beckley's season record. The regional playoff was played at a neutral site, Morris Harvey College in Charleston, West Virginia. It was a dogfight to the end. When the buzzer sounded ending the first round of the state tournament, a sweet feeling of redemption warmed my innards. We were victorious, 71–68. Payback!

We traveled to Morgantown for the second round of the tournament. We were pitted against East Bank High School, who had an outstanding forward by the name of Jerry West. In the first half, we were sluggish and not able to execute well, falling behind by eighteen points. The second half was a different story. We came out strong, outplaying East Bank. With under a minute to play, we had possession of the ball and were down two points with score 73–75. I called a time-out to set the play. My starting point guard had fouled out of the game and was replaced by his backup. Since my two big men, Akers and Blankenship, had been able to score at will, I gave the message in the huddle for the team to take its time and work the ball to either one. We came out of the huddle with a play intact.

After in-bounding the ball, my point guard dribbled around for a couple of seconds and then moved to the foul line and proceeded to do what coaches have nightmares about: he carried out his own play. I watched in amazement as he took the two-point shot ... and missed. East Bank got the rebound, pushed it up the floor, and West scored as the buzzer sounded. Final score: Mullens 73, East Bank 77. We headed home.

That tournament game bothered me for a long time, especially since I was unable to devise a defense that would have slowed down Jerry West. He scored forty-four points in that game. The game replayed over and over in my mind as I questioned my strategies, trying to determine if there was something I could have done differently. After I watched Jerry West play at West Virginia University, where no one slowed him down, and after I watched him play in the NBA, where no one slowed him down, I didn't feel so bad anymore.

That year, the state's well-known high school stars—Jerry West, Willie Akers, and my nephew Butch Goode, the son of Kat and Paul, who was an outstanding ballplayer for Pineville High School—received basketball scholarships to West Virginia University for following year. During their junior year in high school, they had met at Boys State and become good friends. They made a pact that they would attend the same college. As promised, they enrolled in West Virginia University, each receiving a four-year basketball scholarship. Their 1959 team made it to the finals of the NCAA Basketball Championship, the first time in West Virginia sports history. Unfortunately, they lost the championship game to the California Golden Bears by one point. Butch loved to brag about his basketball successes to his cousins Danny and Mike. The day he boasted that he had a NCAA finals wristwatch and wanted to know what college hardware his cousin's had, Mike quickly quipped, "Okay, Butchie, we agree, you got a watch. *Plus* you definitely had the best *seat* in the final NCAA championship game!"

Chapter Eighteen:

1960s to Early 1970s

I had a ten-year hiatus from coaching when I became principal at Mullens High School. I needed to earn a higher salary, as I had a family of four and my teaching salary and coaches' stipend together paid about $3,200 a year. The new job made it easier to raise my family, but it also meant I could not coach Danny or Mike. Well, let's say I couldn't coach them on the floor. To make up for this, I sat in the stands and took copious notes at every ball game, watching every movement and play of their game. There were no video playbacks available in the '50s and '60s, so the only way games were reviewed was through notes. Captioning on paper what was happening on the floor was critical for coaching, and I had a lot of experience. After every ball game, Danny, Mike and I would sit at the kitchen table and review and discuss the notes. I remember one game where Danny had scored forty-two points and Mullens had beaten the other team pretty badly. Danny, I guess, assumed there would be no powwow that night due to his outstanding play. So when I sat down at the table and pulled out my tablet full of notes, he was startled. "Gosh, Dad," Danny exclaimed, "I thought I did pretty well tonight."

I responded, "You did well, but you still made mistakes. You can always improve your play, but that will not happen by ignoring your mistakes. So if you are interested, we can go over tonight's game." In agreement, Danny sat down with me to discuss the game.

Danny and Mike's basketball work ethic in high school paid off for them both. During Danny's senior year in high school, Coach Ellis Johnson from Marshall University visited Wyoming County to recruit players. Coach Johnson, a former player at Kentucky for legendary Coach Adolph Rupp, was Marshall's new head basketball coach and was scouting Dallas Blankenship, an outstanding player from county rival Pineville High School. While sitting in the stands watching Dallas play, Coach Johnson was told by a spectator that he also should look at Danny D'Antoni, a kid from Mullens who was playing on the other team. After he scouted the game, both Danny and Dallas were offered basketball scholarships to Marshall for the upcoming year.

In the early '60s, Marshall University's basketball program was mediocre. Upon Danny's arrival in 1966, the team's record that year was three wins and twenty-three losses. In fact, Marshall had not had a winning season in three years. Because of the freshman recruits by Coach Ellis Johnson, a phenomenal basketball era for Marshall began. The accomplishments of the 1967–69 basketball teams gave the small university national recognition.

The starting nucleus for the 1967 basketball team was nicknamed "The Iron Five." They earned the name because Coach Johnson rarely substituted for them. Danny was the starting point guard for the team. The other four starters were Bob Redd, George Stone, Jim Davidson, and Bob Allen. This group of players was responsible for changing the face of the Marshall University basketball program.

During the late '60s, the National Invitational Tournament (NIT) was a very prestigious college basketball tournament. At that time, the NCAA college basketball tournament invited fewer teams to participate in their tournament, so playing in the NIT was closely akin to securing a berth in today's NCAA tournament.

The Iron Five team not only played in the National Invitational Tournament (NIT) twice during its three-year tenure at Marshall, they were also featured on national television when they played the University of Houston. One member of the Houston team was basketball superstar Elvin Hayes, and they were ranked as the number one college basketball team in the nation. Marshall's Iron Five almost accomplished a huge upset, as they were within four points of being victorious in the waning moments of that game.

At the1967 NIT tournament, which was held at old Madison Square Garden, Marshall played against the University of Nebraska and set the college scoring record of 128 points at the Garden. In the same game, Danny had 18 assists and set the record for the most assists in a single college NIT game. He scored 24 points and gathered 9 rebounds, only one rebound away from a triple-double. Subsequently, the building that housed Madison Square Garden was torn down to make way for the new one, so Danny's record will stand forever in old Madison Square Garden history. In 1996, Danny was inducted into the Marshall Sports Hall of Fame.

In sports, there are celebratory highs when victory is achieved and there are difficult lows when suffering a loss, but to encounter both is not only unusual, it's extremely unpleasant. With all the basketball games going on in the D'Antoni lives, it was inevitable that Mike and Danny would play in two different major basketball events on the same night. In 1968, Betty Jo, Mark, and I were staying at the Holiday Inn in Charleston. We were there to attend the West Virginia state basketball championship tournament being held at the Civic Center. Mike was playing in the tournament, and we were preparing to go to the game. At 7:00 PM, about an hour before Mike's game, Betty Jo turned on the television so we could watch the first round of the National Invitational Basketball Tournament (NIT), which Danny was playing in. For the second year in a row, the Marshall Thundering Herd had been invited to participate in the prestigious tournament in New York, so the excitement in our family was at a double intensity. The local newspaper had sent a photographer to our room to take pictures of our family. They were doing a human interest story on the D'Antonis and the two games. Reportedly, the headline was to read: THE NIGHT TO REMEMBER. They took a picture of Betty Jo, Mark, and I standing in front of the television that was currently broadcasting Danny's game. Danny was having a great game, and the Thundering Herd took a twenty-one point lead into halftime. Thinking everything was under control with the Marshall game, we headed with high expectations to Mike's game at the Civic Center.

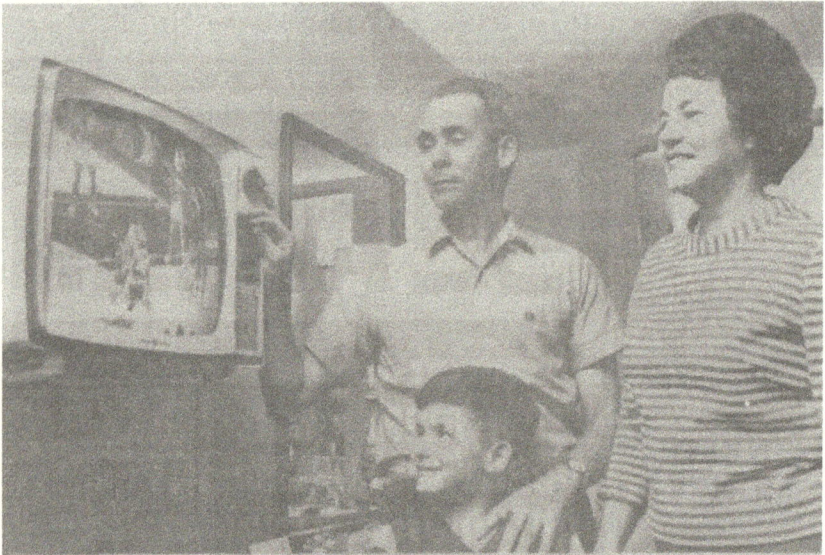

NON-PLAYING D'ANTONIS . . Lewis, Wife And Son Mark

Newspaper Article on the Night to Forget

The Mullens Rebels were pitted against Charles Town High School in the semifinal round of the state tournament. The game was a dogfight, and when it ended, Mullens had lost by two points. Disappointed for Mike and his team, we had hopes that Danny had been successful. Hurrying back to our hotel room, we turned on the television to watch the evening's sporting news. Within minutes, we knew that the article entitled "A Night to Remember" would change to read "A Night to Forget." Marshall had blown their twenty-one point lead and lost to St. Peter's College on a last-second shot.

In 1969, the year Mike graduated from high school, I was offered a job out of the state at Chesapeake High School as head basketball coach and assistant principal. The opportunity came at the right time. At the time of the offer, I was eligible for retirement from the West Virginia school system. Chesapeake, Ohio, was located directly across the Ohio River from Huntington, West Virginia, home of Marshall University, where Mike had accepted a basketball scholarship and Danny was the freshman basketball coach. Starting the new job meant I would return to coaching, my passion, and that I would be ten minutes away from Mike's college games. It may have taken me all of five minutes to accept the job.

Mike's Signing at Marshall University (L-R Betty Jo, Danny, Mark, Mike, Lewis and Coach Johnson

Following in the 1967–69 Marshall basketball dynasty's footsteps, another great Marshall team emerged, and Mike was the starting point guard. Mike was recruited by over 150 college teams, and after much discussion and debate, made the decision to attend Marshall. I think the deciding factor was his brother, Danny, who had been hired as the freshman basketball coach for the 1970 recruits. For the first time in their lives, Mike and Danny were on the same basketball team. Their freshman record was nine wins and three losses.

In the three seasons that followed at Marshall, Mike, as the playmaker guard, led the Thundering Herd to a 59–21 overall record and to berths in both the NCAA (1971–72 season) and NIT (1972–73 season) postseason tournaments. He helped the 1971–72 team reach a national ranking of eighth in the Associated Press poll. This was the highest ranking in school history at the Division 1 level. Subsequently, Mike was inducted into the Marshall Sports Hall of Fame and his number 10 jersey was retired. Both Danny and Mike's team brought national recognition to the Marshall University basketball program, and they have debated for years which one had the better team.

In my opinion, the greatest accomplishment for their Marshall teams was not the victories or the individual records that were posted, it was the reaction of the community and how it emerged as a family unit to support the teams. The basketball teams' family spirit overflowed into the town and captured the hearts of the people of Huntington, West Virginia, and created a dynamic and compelling Marshall family that bonded the town and university. The entire populace of Huntington embraced the college team, and as a result, a winning spirit was established. The sense of family permeated every fiber of the college, and winners were created. The night Marshall's basketball team defeated Nebraska at the NIT, setting a national record, the entire town celebrated. As the buzzer sounded ending the televised game, thousands of people in Huntington poured onto the city streets, stopping traffic, singing and dancing, all rejoicing in the accomplishment of their team, their family.

But life's cycle does not always allow for rejoicing. At times, life is unfair, not right, and delivers unfathomable news. In 1970, the Marshall family suffered the ultimate tragedy. On November 22, 1970, a rainy fall night, fate struck a cruel blow that reverberated across the state of West Virginia. Seventy Marshall family members perished in a horrible plane crash while returning home from a football game against East Carolina. The crash was labeled the worst air disaster in American sports history. The country, the state, the community, and individuals all lost family members, close friends, and an entire generation of visionary Marshall leaders that ill-fated night.

The loss was excruciating for the community of Huntington, the children of the families left behind, to my family, and to me. Among the passengers on the ill-fated plane was Head Coach Ricky Tolley, an outstanding young man who played ball for me at Mullens High School. I also grieved for Dr. Ray Hagley and his wife Shirley, two very close friends who were responsible for me becoming the head coach at Chesapeake High School.

Today, the scars still remain deep and raw. Time has eased the searing pain that gripped the community that night, but the silencing of these voices and spirits still haunts the Marshall family unit.

Chapter Nineteen:

Coaching a Son

While at Chesapeake High School, I finally got the opportunity to coach one of my sons, Mark. Coaching Danny and Mike was denied to me because I became a principal of the school instead of a coach in order to better support my family. It is the one thing in my life that I wish could have been different, but by coaching Mark, I was finely able to experience and enjoy what was earlier denied to me.

Mark, my point guard, was a very smart player who always gave 100 percent and knew how to take advantage of situations that arose on the basketball court. He was a talented ballplayer and made coaching much easier, even though Mark at times wondered if I even liked him.

During Mark's junior year, our basketball team was mediocre. We had potential, but the team as a whole was not completely developed. My philosophy on the critical role of the point guard meant Mark became the primary target in practice. In Mark's eyes, I was being overly critical, and he felt he could not do anything right. In my eyes, it was an attempt to develop his talents to the fullest.

Coming home one night from practice, I was met at the door by Betty Jo, who informed me that I had a son who was in his bedroom crying. She said he felt that I didn't like him and that he was a terrible ballplayer. She informed me that I needed to address the situation. And, of course, when Betty Jo expressed an adamant request, it was followed.

I entered Mark's bedroom knowing I had some explaining to do. He was a great kid, a straight-A student who never created a problem for us, and was a terrific ballplayer. I needed to convey to him that my "picking" on him was not to hurt him but was meant to make him a better basketball player. Plus, he was in the unfortunate position of being the starting point guard for his father's team. That translated into everyone's eyes paying attention to how he was treated and what was expected of him by his coach. Unfortunately, he had to either be the best player on the team or to endure the behind-the-back snickers and hurtful comments that come from this type of situation. Walking into his room, my heart hurt as I looked into my son's tearful eyes and his sad expression.

"Mark, do you have a problem you want to share with me?"

"Not really," Mark mumbled.

"Well, if you don't have a problem, maybe you can help me solve my problem," I remarked.

Mark looked up at me. "You have a problem?"

"Yes, I do, and I am trying my very best to work through it. I think our basketball team has a shot at a state championship, and I have just the right person at the point guard position to help me get them there. The other positions on the team are important too, but to me, the point guard is the key to every winning basketball team. It is the position that drives the unit, energizes the play, sees the big picture, and makes basketball stars out of the other players. But to get the team to where it needs to be, the point guard must almost be perfect on the court, and so my job is to make sure the point guard can be the best he can be. So, here is the problem: do I let some of the mistakes that I see go by without comment, which I could easily do, and we could still have a good season, or do I continue to correct the point guard's play, helping him improve, and, as a result, have a great basketball season? What do you think I should do?"

Mark thought a minute, and as the inborn D'Antoni competitive spirit rose from the depths of his heartache, he answered me, "Go after the point guard, Dad!"

Thinking about this now, I guess I did require my children to be the best they could be, to lay it all out there, and then to accept the outcome of their endeavors with dignity and resolve.

It was great that Mark has shared in the success of the basketball team at Chesapeake High School. During my tenure, the basketball teams were able to win six Ohio Valley Conference Championships. Mark was a member of two of those teams.

Along the way, there were two unusual basketball games. The first was the only five-overtime game I coached. We were playing against South Point High School. It seemed like no one wanted to win the game, as both teams played poorly. It took us five overtimes and most of the starters on both teams fouling out before we finally won.

The second game was one of our best games. It was the night we beat Peeples High School, the team picked to win the Ohio high school basketball tournament that year. We came into Peeples High School that evening as the extreme underdog. Peeples was ranked number one in Ohio and was the odds-on favorite for winning the state basketball championship. As my team filed into the gym area in route to the locker rooms, I noted, as did all my players, that the gym was overflowing with loud hometown fans. They had come out in record numbers to cheer for their championship-bound team. In contrast, our side only had a handful of loyal fans who had traveled to the ballgame.

Thinking about the difference that would be heard from the crowd's reaction as the two teams entered the gym, I got an idea. Hurrying my team into the locker room, I told them to dress quickly. Once they were ready, I held them in a line at the door of the locker room and told them not to move until I gave them the signal to run onto the floor. Next, I instructed our team manager to watch the Peeples locker room. I told him to let me know immediately when the Peeples team opened the door to run onto the floor. Within minutes, our manager gave me the sign. I immediately opened our locker room door and sent my team out. Both teams entered the gym floor at the same time and received the same standing and very loud ovation. We beat Peeples that night, recording one of the largest upsets in Ohio high school basketball chronicles.

My time as a coach was coming to an end, and it was wonderful that among the for last games of my coaching career, my son was the point guard of the team. During Mark's senior year, we had a great team. Close to reaching our goal to become the Ohio State high school champions, we met Portsmouth High School on a neutral site. Portsmouth also had a good team that year, but I thought and still do think that we had the better team. It was a very close game with the winner was determined in the final minutes.

With approximately two minutes left in the game, the refs made two questionable calls. The first was a three-second lane violation called on one of my players, and the second was a charging foul called on Mark, fouling him out of the game. Those two calls sealed our fate, and we lost to Portsmouth that night. Portsmouth went on to play in the finals of the Ohio state championship. Personally, I think we got a little bit of "home cooking" that night as both refs were from Portsmouth. Betty Jo, where were you when I needed you?

After graduation, Mark attended Coastal Carolina College in Myrtle Beach, South Carolina, on a four-year basketball scholarship and later fulfilled his mother's dream by becoming a prominent lawyer in West Virginia.

At the end of the 1981 basketball season, at the age of sixty-seven, I checked in my tennis shoes, whistle, and clipboard. Saying good-bye to coaching was difficult, but I knew it was time to leave, as Betty Jo threatened divorce if I did not retire and return with her to our home in Mullens.

Back in Mullens, Betty Jo and I continued our lives in the retirement. We traveled a little, and I even convinced Betty Jo, who hated airplane travel, to fly to Denver to spend Christmas with Mike, his wife Laurel, and our grandson, Michael, as they had moved from Italy back to the States, where Mike had accepted a job with the Denver Nuggets as head of player personnel.

During these years, our family continued to grow, and we had the wonderful pleasure of being blessed with eight beautiful grandchildren, Matthew, Andrew, Nicholas, Morgan, Bailey, Parker, Kennedy, and Michael. Betty Jo and I visited our children and grandchildren whenever possible. Jokingly, as the number of grandchildren began to grow, Betty Jo told her children, "Be sure and blow the horn when you drive by the house so I can come out and see what the grandchildren look like." The comment became the standing household joke as the family numbers continued to grow at each new family gathering.

Years later, it was a Saturday night. We had just finished a game of bridge earlier that evening and were preparing for bed when the unthinkable happened: Betty Jo became very ill. I called 911 for help. Betty Jo had suffered a massive stroke.

After fifty-seven short—very short—years of marriage, our life together on earth came to a close. Betty Jo's life ended on December 9, 1998, when she was only seventy-seven years old. A large part of me died that day with her. She was the love of my life, the fun, the joy, the spark that lit up the room. The large oak table that holds the porcelain chicken containing the family-favorite recipes still remains in her kitchen, the coffee pot still perks, guests are still welcome, but the magic she created is gone, and the chair where she sat and held court for fifty-plus years is empty. Drawing strength from my dad's lessons, I held together and forced myself to move forward. But, Betty Jo, my love and my best friend, is sorely missed.

Chapter Twenty:

Return to the Homeland

In 2002, Mike and Laurel gave me a wonderful gift. They took me on my first visit to Italy and to Campi, where my mother and father were born. I have to say that traveling through Italy with Mike as the guide was quite an experience. He is an icon in Italy. I knew he was successful as a player and coach because he had won numerous national and European championships and awards. Even knowing that he was selected the top point guard of all time in the Italian professional league and was named one of the top fifty players in European professional basketball, I still had no clue as to the depth and breadth of his popularity until we made the trip. Everywhere we went in the country, we were greeted and treated like royalty. Fans pursued him for autographs and pictures, businesses and restaurants opened their doors to him, and even I, as his father, got special treatment. It was unbelievable.

Traveling to Venice, we went to dinner at a local family restaurant. The owner, who recognized Mike and was thrilled that he had chosen his restaurant to dine in, served us wild boar, the specialty of the house. The meal was presented to us as a gift from the owner. Not wanting to insult anyone, I agreed to try the delicacy. I don't remember much after the dinner, as dizziness overcame me, and the rest of the evening developed into a blur. I know I made it to my hotel room, but that was the end of my memory of that day. Sometimes it does not pay to be a celebrity.

Continuing our trip, we toured Rome and then ventured up the mountains to visit the town of Assisi. The next day, we arrived in Campi, my father and mother's birthplace, and I was amazed by its physical resemblance to Mullens and West Virginia. The small town, the mountains, the rustic way of life that surrounded my parents when they lived in Italy must have transcended to their new home in West Virginia and helped them feel at home in their adopted country.

In Campi, we entered a local bar to inquire about my parents' home. Opening the door, we were met with curious stares, as our small group did not look like locals. Thank goodness Mike and Laurel spoke Italian, as no one seemed to speak English. We were given the directions to where my parents lived but were told that Dad's home no longer stood. It was torn down a couple of years prior.

Arriving at my mother's home, I surveyed the area. Next door was the vacant lot where my dad's house had once stood. Standing there, I experienced an eerie sensation that spread through my body. The stark reality became crystal clear. My folks had been very, very poor and had endured many hardships. In contrast, here I stood on their soil, rich in every aspect of my life because of them and their fierce determination to succeed. They had made it happen for me. The thought was almost overwhelming as the love and gratitude for my parents pumped through my veins.

Word of our visit to Campi reached the ears of the mayor of Norchia, the province of Campi, and he extended an initiation for us to visit his office. The next day, we found a surprise when we met with the mayor. Dressed in full mayoral garb, he presented me with the Key to the Province of Norchia in honor of my parents. It was a moment I will always remember. I hope Mom and Dad were watching over us, as the tribute was in their honor.

Memories from Italy

Memories from Italy

Memories from Italy

Memories from Italy

Chapter Twenty-one:

Closing Thoughts

My retirement years continue to be active and exciting. At eighty-nine, I was given the West Virginia Distinguished Citizen Award by the governor; at the age of ninety, I made my first hole in one on my home golf course and was inducted into the West Virginia Sports Hall of Fame; and at the age of ninety-five, I received our town's Distinguished Citizen of the Year Award and was the grand marshal in the local Christmas parade. With all that said (other than the hole in one, which I thought was about time considering all the golf I have played in my lifetime), one wonders if the awards presented in the latter part of my life are due to my age, my children's accomplishments, or my own true merit. In retrospect, I have decided to remain appreciative, to respect them for the face value, and leave the whole deep philosophical meanderings to those who will take the opportunity to decide.

My children and their children are amazing, and I am so proud to continue to play a role in their lives. I am happy to say that they continue to respect my father's vow that the name D'Antoni will always carry honor. My prayer, and hopefully my legacy, is that my father's wish will continue for generations to come.

Sitting on my porch surrounded by the West Virginia mountains showing off their vibrant fall colors, I think about my family and its history that is laced with Italian and American accents. A thought lingers in my mind as I become aware of an eerie coincidence that marks my father's entry at Ellis Island with my sons' trip to Madison Square Garden in New York City to coach the New York Knicks. The similarities are staggering. My father arrived in New York through Ellis Island one hundred years nearly to the day that his grandsons arrived in New York to coach at Madison Square Garden. Andrea, my father, was an Italian citizen seeking American citizenship. His grandson Mike lived and worked in both countries and has dual citizenship. My father initially spoke only Italian but learned English as an adult. As an adult, Mike speaks both languages fluently. My dad arrived in the United States with a life full of unknown challenges and much uncertainty, whereas professional life as a Knick consists of the same.

Some may say it is Italian superstition, but my heart and my head tell me that Andrea is guiding my children as they face their own uncertainties. My concern for their welfare is tempered by the knowledge that Dad's experience and wisdom that he so wisely endowed to me is continuing its cycle as my children's lives continue to evolve and their roles in their own family units are developed and expanded. I am so blessed that my father gave us the presence of life and that I am able to bestow my own children with the same gift.

My final thoughts as I close yet another adventure in my life are written specifically for young people who are still trying to decide how to live their lives. To them, I say the journey is what gives you the great ride, and to travel with family is what makes it a fulfilling trip. Not only are there others to celebrate with you or to console you, but you are part of their celebrations as well. And finally, success first begins with the thought of *I can*. The secret to a winning life is the same secret that produces a winning basketball team, and it was revealed to me by my father almost a hundred years ago: *all is determined by how well you prepare and how you choose to react to the ebb and flow of the play.*

Afterword by Kathy D'Antoni

Lewis Joseph D'Antoni, my father, continues to reside in Mullens, West Virginia. He spends his days reading, watching sports on TV, surfing the Internet, playing bridge on the weekends, and cooking spaghetti dinners for his friends.

Dad spends his winters in New York and can be seen sitting behind the Knicks bench at all their home games until March, when he returns to his home.

Being a very humble and modest man, Dad did not go into great detail about the accomplishments of his life, so I will, as I think they should be told. The following is an abbreviated account of his honors:

Achievements earned while attending Concord College:

- Elected president of the freshmen class
- Elected president of Phi Delta Pi fraternity
- Lettered four years in football
- Lettered four years in basketball
- Lettered in tennis

- Named WVIAC All-Conference Football Team—1936
- Named WVIAC All-Tournament Basketball Team—1935, 1936
- Was leading scorer in basketball for four years
- Named captain of football team—1936
- Named captain of basketball team—1936
- Selected to the All-Time WVIAC Football and Basketball Team
- Joined Blue Key Fraternity

Achievements earned after leaving Concord College:

- Played Class D Baseball with the Bluefield Blue Grays—1938, .369 batting average
- Served forty-four months as chief specialist and LT.JG in the navy during World War II
- Served fifteen months in the Pacific aboard LST 585 as a gunnery officer
- Started six-man football program at Pineville High School—1938
- Named Mullens High School football coach—1946–50
- Earned record of 26–18
- Named Pineville basketball coach—1937–41
- Earned record of 59–45
- Named Mullens High School basketball coach—1942–59
- Earned record of 223–75
- Selected as assistant baseball coach of South All-Stars—1951
- Selected head baseball coach of South All-Stars—1952
- Selected as West Virginia High School All-Stars head coach and played the Kentucky High School All- Stars—1955
- Participated in five state basketball tournaments
- Named West Virginia High School State Runner-up Basketball Champions—1954

- Won West Virginia High School State Basketball Championship—1955
- Selected as West Virginia High School Coach of the Year—1955
- Selected Area Basketball Coach of the Year—1947, '51, and '55
- Started the Little League and Babe Ruth League in Mullens
- Earned a career basketball coaching record of 450 wins and 200 losses

Achievements earned after relocating as head basketball coach at Chesapeake High School in Ohio:

- Won Ohio Valley Conference- six years
- Selected as Ohio Valley Conference Coach of the Year six times
- Selected as head coach of Ohio Valley High School All-Stars—1980, '82
- Won both years as head coach of the Ohio Valley All-Stars

Achievements in Retirement:

- Presented with Distinguished West Virginian Award by Governor Caperton—1992
- Inducted into the West Virginia Sportswriter's Hall of Fame
- Selected as Retired Coach of the Year by the West Virginia High School Coaches Association
- Selected as a Charter Member of the Concord College Hall of Fame—September 30, 1995
- Named to WVIACC All-Time Teams for basketball and football

- Inducted into Chesapeake High School Athletic Hall of Fame
- Inducted into Mullens High School Hall of Fame

Contributions to the Town of Mullens:

- Worked with other members of the community to get a recreation levy passed in Mullens that resulted in four playgrounds, two tennis courts, and a swimming pool
- Managed the athletic field and playgrounds during the summer months
- Organized and ran the pickup basketball leagues for fifteen years, which were played on the outdoor playground basketball courts every night during the summer
- Director of the marble tournaments held in Mullens area
- Organized Mullens Little League
- Organized Babe Ruth League in Mullens
- Took care of the baseball field during the summer— including clean up of bleachers and grounds
- Provided financial scholarships to Mullens' high school students from his scholarship fund, established in his honor at his eightieth birthday party

And the most outstanding achievement:

- **Lewis has mentored thousands of students who have achieved successful lives.**

www.ingramcontent.com/pod-product-compliance
Lightning Source LLC
Chambersburg PA
CBHW021102090426
42738CB00006B/467